Nature Walks in Central Massachusetts

An AMC Nature Walks Book

Michael Tougias
René Laubach

APPALACHIAN MOUNTAIN CLUB BOOKS
BOSTON, MASSACHUSETTS

Cover Photograph: Broad Meadow Brook, Michael Tougias
All photographs by the authors unless otherwise noted.
Book & Cover Design: Carol Bast Tyler

Distributed by the Globe Pequot Press, Inc., Old Saybrook, CT

Library of Congress Cataloging-in-Publication Data

The paper used in this publication meets the minimum requirements of the
American National Standard for Information Sciences—Permanence of
Paper for Printed Library Materials, ANSI Z39.48–1984.∞

**Due to changes in conditions,
use of the information in this book
is at the sole risk of the user.**

Printed on recycled paper using soy-based inks.
Printed in the United States of America.

10 9 8 7 6 5 4 3 2 1   96 97 98 99 00 01

Contents

Locations of Walks

VERMONT

BERKSHIRE COUNTY

MT. GRACE S.F.

MOHAWK TRAIL S.F.

112

NORTHFIELD MTN.

2

HIGH
LEDGES

ERVING S.F.

DUBUQUE S.F.

Greenfield

BEAR SWAMP RES.

WENDELL S.F.

9

W.C. BRYANT
HOMESTEAD

CHAPELBROOK

BEAR'S DE

D.A.R. S.F.

MT. SUGARLOAF S.R.

I-91

Connecticut
River

143

BUFFAM FALLS

CHESTERFIELD GORGE

Quabbin
Reservoir

GLENDALE FALLS

Northampton

9

112

ARCADIA W.S.

SKINNER S.P.

MT. TOM S.R.

HOLYOKE RANGE S.P.

SANDERSON BROOK FALLS

I-90

TOLLAND S.F.

Springfield

57

LAUGHING BROOK

GRANVILLE S.F.

THE MEADOWS

in this Book

Acknowledgments

A great number of people helped with this book, and we sincerely thank them for sharing their time and knowledge. In particular we would like to thank Dick O'Brien and Paul Grzgbowski, who supervise the central region reservations for The Trustees of Reservations; Don Reid, Western Regional Ecologist for The Trustees of Reservations; Jeanne Anderson, Doug Kimball, Tom Tyning, and Ron Wolanin of Massachusetts Audubon Society; Dutch Barnard; Simon Geary; and Bob and Johnie Leverett for their knowledge, advice, and assistance. Also a note of appreciation to our editor, Gordon Hardy, and his ability to bring a manuscript to a higher level and still allow the individual writer's style to flourish.

Lastly, we would like to thank our families for joining us on walks, and then giving us the time to work on the manuscript. René wishes to thank especially his wife, Christyna, for being a wonderful companion and a great help in the field.

Introduction

A WEEKEND is just not a weekend without a walk in the woods. The physical joy of walking combined with the potential of seeing wildlife make for a winning combination. A special day outdoors can make your spirits soar. Maybe it's a walk on a crisp, colorful autumn day, or a winter's trek just after a heavy snow, or perhaps the first warm day of spring when all the earth seems to be awakening.

Central Massachusetts affords a number of diverse pockets of wilderness where you can walk in solitude. Properties range in size from the few acres around the waterfall at Bear's Den to the sprawling forests protecting Quabbin Reservoir. One of our toughest challenges was deciding which of the 100 or so properties we researched to include in the 42 reviewed in the book. Ultimately the selection was narrowed down to include properties that had the most diversity. There are hilltop overlooks, quaking cedar bogs, riverfront trails, glacial eskers and erratics, and walks that will take you by lesser-known historic sites.

Each location review includes directions, suggested trails, a map, wildlife and plants to be seen, estimated hiking time, trail conditions, and scenic views. If there is a nearby point of interest we give a brief description and directions. The initials at the end of each section indicate whether it was written by Michael Tougias (M.T.) or René Laubach (R.L.).

We have also included a level of difficulty for each walk. In general we have rated walks under three miles on fairly level terrain as *easy* and walks of three miles or more as *medium*. Walks that are over five miles or go up steep hills are rated as *difficult*.

Thoreau viewed walking as a way to lose oneself: "What business have I in the woods, if I am thinking of something out of the woods?" He walked often and far afield: "I think that I cannot preserve my health and spirits, unless I spend four hours a day at least—and it is commonly more than that—sauntering through the woods and over the hills and fields, absolutely free from all worldly engagements." And if Thoreau saw wildlife, all the better. It was not unusual for him to sit and wait patiently for some creature to appear or to stop his walk to watch wildlife for the rest of the day. Your walks can be more enjoyable if you follow Thoreau's examples.

We wrote this book to share some of our special places with you and hope that by raising appreciation for nature we can protect more wild places before they are forever lost to development.

A few suggestions

- To make your hikes more enjoyable bring binoculars, a camera, water, and a snack (food tastes better in the outdoors).
- Bring extra film—we always seem to run out when the best picture presents itself.
- Unfortunately it's not advisable for women to hike alone. Ask a friend who shares your love of the out-

doors, or better yet, pick a friend who spends more time in the malls than the woods, and introduce him or her to the joys of walking in the great out-doors.

- Getting lost in the woods is no fun. If you are unfamiliar with an area be sure to allow plenty of time before dark when you set out. Even at the smaller properties it's possible to get lost. Always tell some-one what properties you plan to explore.

- The tiny ticks that can carry Lyme disease are spread nearly throughout New England. Always wear long pants, preferably with the pants tucked beneath your socks. Use bug repellent on your skin, socks, and pants. Avoid fields of tall grass during the warm-weather months. And to be on the safe side, give yourself a "tick check" after every hike by examining yourself all over, especially the scalp, neck, armpits, groin, and ankles. The most common initial symptoms of Lyme disease include swollen lymph nodes near the site of the bite, flulike symp-toms, and a rash around site of the bite. The rash expands from the center out, and it may look like a bull's-eye.

- Be on the lookout for poison ivy—identified by its three shiny leaves. Again, long pants are recom-mended.

- During warm-weather months carry a small back-pack or fanny pack with water and bug spray. (It's a good idea to have a pack permanently loaded for nature walks, so that all you need do is fill the water bottle.)

- During cold-weather months layer your clothes, so

that you can peel off or add items easily. The best
layering is a moisture-wicking inner layer, a warm
insulating middle layer, and a waterproof/wind-
proof outer layer. Be sure to wear warm, water-
proof boots. Always bring a hat.

- Deer hunting season is in the fall; wear a blaze
orange hat to be on the safe side—even when in a
no-hunting area.
- Learn how to use a map and compass—there are
several good introductory books and workshops
available through the AMC and other organizations. Bring them along on your hikes.

Trail courtesy

Respect for nature involves a few basic rules.

- Be sure to follow the "carry-in, carry-out" principle
when it comes to trash. If you want to be an extra-
good citizen, carry along a small trash bag and col-
lect litter left by less thoughtful individuals.
- Do not remove any plants or animals from the
woods. Return logs and rocks that you move to
their original positions.
- Keep to the established trails.
- Give wildlife a wide berth. Binoculars (7 – 10 x 40)
and a telephoto lens on your camera will allow you
to view the wildlife without forcing it to flee.

By becoming involved in local conservation efforts, we
can all help to keep our woods and waters in a clean,
natural state, where wildlife has a chance to flourish.

Besides local conservation commissions and watershed associations, there are also regional and statewide organizations such as the Appalachian Mountain Club, The Trustees of Reservations, and Massachusetts Audubon Society that have active conservation programs.

Wildlife watching

The reservations, sanctuaries, and conservation lands reviewed in this book are all rich in wildlife. Seeing that wildlife, however, depends on both luck and one's knowledge of the creatures themselves. We can't do much about luck, but there are a number of steps that can be taken to increase your odds of spotting the many birds, mammals, amphibians, and insects that live in central Massachusetts.

Thoreau was an expert "wildlife watcher," patient and full of curiosity. He would think nothing of sitting for an hour to watch a bird or animal gather food. "True men of science," he wrote, "will know nature better by his finer organizations; he will smell, taste, see, hear, feel, better than other men. His will be a deeper and finer experience." Nature reveals more of her subtleties when we focus all our senses into the natural surroundings. Try following Thoreau's example and let yourself become absorbed by the forests, fields, and water—even if you don't see wildlife, the walks themselves are more rewarding and refreshing.

Two of the key components of wildlife watching are knowing where and when to look. The best time to see most wildlife is at dawn and dusk. Many creatures are nocturnal, and there is also some overlap at dawn and dusk with the daytime birds and animals. Spring and fall are the two best seasons, especially for migratory birds. Animals that hibernate will be active during the spring after a long winter, and in the fall they will eat as much as possible in preparation for the cold months to come. Winter has the least activity but it does offer some advantages, such as easier long-range viewing (no foliage), easily visible tracks in fresh snow, the potential to see some animals crossing the ice (such as coyotes); also animals are often easier to spot against a background of white snow.

Experienced wildlife watchers look everywhere: in the fields, on the forest floor, under logs and stones, on the water or ice, along shorelines, in trees, and in the sky. Perhaps the single most productive spot for seeing wildlife is the edge of a field. Hawks and owls often perch here, and many animals make their dens and burrows where the woods meet the meadows. Creatures feel safer around the edges—deer often stay close to these fringe areas before entering a field at nightfall. Red fox and coyotes hunt the edges, and they can sometimes be seen trotting through tall grass on their rounds.

Other productive areas are along riverbanks and shorelines. Mink, weasels, muskrat, and raccoons, just to mention a few, are commonly observed foraging next to water. And of course shorebirds, wading birds, and ducks are found here. Scanning a shoreline with a pair of binoculars can be extremely rewarding—you may see a number of different wildlife species. Many of the wild areas in this book offer excellent canoeing, and this, too, affords opportunities for nature study at close range.

Obviously, when walking through the woods you must do so quietly if you hope to get near wildlife, but being quiet is not enough. Most creatures would prefer to hide than run, and they will sit tight and let you walk right by. You should give the surrounding areas more than a casual glance. For example, when trying to spot deer, look for parts of the animal between the trees rather than for the entire body. Look for the horizontal lines of the deer's back contrasting with the vertical trees. Knowing the size of the animal also helps; when scanning for deer most people would do so at eye level, yet deer are only about three feet high at the shoulder.

Many animals blend in with their surroundings so well it's almost impossible to see them. The American bittern, for example, sometimes hides by freezing with its head and long neck in an upright position to match tall reeds and vegetation around it. A snapping turtle in shallow water looks just like a rock, and ruffed grouse can be indistinguishable from the fallen leaves on the forest floor. Even great blue herons will stop feeding and wait, silent and unmoving, until perceived danger passes.

Another key factor to consider is wind direction, which can carry your scent to wildlife. As you walk down a trail try looking upwind—animals will detect your scent on your downwind side. If you have a choice when beginning a hike, travel into the wind. The same holds true when approaching a known feeding area. Serious wildlife photographers even go as far as wearing rubber boots to stop the scent from their feet from escaping into the air!

It is important, by the way, that we humans do not approach creatures too closely. Birds will take wing and animals will run away, thus expending valuable energy to avoid us. If you keep your distance many creatures will allow you to observe them, so long as you do not walk directly at them or linger too long.

Some animals are almost never seen because they are nocturnal and secretive. But you don't have to see them to know that they are present. They leave clues. You will find the tracks of otter, heron, raccoon, and deer along the soft margin of a river or lake. Looking for fresh tracks after a snowfall can be especially rewarding. Some astute trackers can also identify creatures by the droppings they leave behind. The burrows and dens of animals reveal where animals such as the fox and groundhog live. Owls disgorge pellets, which can identify their presence and what they have been feeding on. Look for them underneath large pine trees. Deer leave a number of signs: the trails they use between feeding and resting grounds and the scrapes and scars on saplings caused by a buck rubbing its antlers. Peeled bark can mean deer, mice, rabbit, or others, depending on the teeth marks, shape, and height of the marking.

The time and patience required to find and identify clues can be significant, but so too are the rewards. It is satisfying to solve the wildlife "puzzle," not only in learning of a species' presence but to also deduce what its activities were. Children especially enjoy this detective work.

Besides using your eyes, you should use your ears to help in wildlife identification. Learning the songs and calls of birds will greatly enhance your enjoyment of the outdoors. Many of us have heard the hooting of an owl at night or the daytime drumming of the male ruffed grouse. It appears that more and more folks in the outer suburbs will soon be hearing the wild and eerie yapping and howling of coyotes. Some animal sounds are quite surprising. Creatures you wouldn't expect to make a peep can be quite vocal at times. We've heard deer snort, porcupines scream, and woodchucks grunt and click their teeth.

Knowing the behavior of birds and animals can often explain their actions. For example, if a ruffed grouse pulls the "wounded wing act," you can be sure its chicks are near and it is trying to draw you away. The mother grouse makes a commotion, dragging its wing in a way sure to get your attention. After watching the mother's act, take a moment to scan the forest floor and you just might see the chicks (look, but don't touch, and be careful where you step). Some other creatures give warnings if you get too close. A goshawk guarding its nest will give a warning of "kak, kak, kak"; don't go any closer, it may attack you. (Never get too close to nesting birds or chase or corner an animal. Oftentimes the best way to get a second look at an animal is to remain perfectly still. They may return out of curiosity.)

Nature study is all the more fascinating when you learn the habits of each wild animal; what it eats, where and when it feeds and rests, whether it is active in the winter or hibernates. Birds can be studied in a similar way, and of course migration patterns are crucial to understanding when and for how long certain birds are in our region. Amphibians and reptiles are generally only active in the warm-weather months, relying on their behavior and surroundings to control their internal temperatures. The relatively few amphibians and reptiles that live in Massachusetts must overwinter in holes or burrows below the frost line. Some (e.g., wood frog) can survive freezing! The best time to see some of them is in the late spring or early summer (usually June); for example, that's when the snapping turtle comes out of the water to lay its eggs on land.

For wildlife photography, you need a zoom lens and a tripod. High-quality shots are extremely difficult to achieve. It's hard enough just locating an animal or uncommon bird, but finding a clear shot for a picture can be quite frustrating. Patience is the key—that's why professional wildlife photographers often spend days in the woods working from a blind.

Consider searching for "small game." Colorful butterflies nectaring on wildflowers, dragonflies hawking for insects along a pond shore, and red-spotted newts courting at the edge of a beaver pond can be just as fascinating as an encounter with a larger creature. The key is to look closely.

Finally, don't discount dumb luck. Much of wildlife we have seen has been by accident, but we greatly increased our odds by repeat visits to favorite properties.

Nature Walking with Children

A walk in the woods with a child can be a wonderful experience or a potential nightmare! The most important step you can take is simply to be flexible. High expectations can ruin any trip. Be ready to turn back anytime, and don't force your goals on a child. When a child shows signs of fatigue take a rest, then turn back—or you might find yourself carrying the child back to the car. And remember that walking in the snow, sand, or mud can use up twice as much energy as a walk of the same length on hard ground.

We have found that a little preparation goes a long way in ensuring that both adult and child have a good time. Bring a **snack;** oftentimes the child will be more interested in the snack than in the natural world. (There's nothing wrong with that; the idea here is to have fun and make the trip a pleasant one.) Bring a **field guide** to birds, animals, reptiles, and plants (see the recommended list on p. 284).

A guide enables the child to work with you in identifying the natural world around them. **Binoculars** are always a big hit, and if you do spot wildlife, binoculars might allow the child to see much more than a fleeting glimpse. A hand lens can open up a whole new world. Let the child hold the **map,** and have them help decide which way to go while you teach them how to interpret the map. You might also want to purchase the child a **small backpack;** from the child's viewpoint this seems to somehow make the trip more of an adventure, as if you are going to explore some far-off place. Pack a whistle in the child's backpack, and explain that it is to be used (blown at regular intervals) only if the child becomes separated from the parent.

Spending a day outdoors with a child is a great way to become closer and at the same time teach them a respect for nature. You can show them responsibility through your own actions, such as picking up trash—even if it's not yours. Try to see the world through their eyes and enjoy the simple things that feed their enthusiasm. (If the location has water, it's a good bet the child will want to spend some time throwing twigs or stones.) When you take a rest, that's a good time to tell stories about nature or browse through the field guide together. Remember to praise and encourage the child each time he or she learns something new or completes a walk.

Recommended walks with younger children

All the walks rated easy or medium are good for children. Generally, the walks listed here have fairly level terrain and well maintained routes. On a few of the longer walks you should not attempt to do the whole route described in the book but rather a small portion, depending on the age and interest of the child.

Children love to explore rocky ledges, boulders, the edges of ponds and streams, lookouts, wooden footbridges, and observation towers. The following places are personal favorites for introducing youngsters to the natural world:

How to Use this Book

THE WALKS are grouped into three sections according to the counties they are in. (See the locator map before the introduction.) Once you have selected the location you want to explore, and have read the property description, look up directions to the site under "Getting There," found at the end of each walk.

The approximate time it takes to make the recommended walk is given at the beginning of each entry, as well as the level of difficulty. The time-to-mileage ratio used is about 30 minutes for each mile, but if you're like us you will want to allow more time to enjoy the environment. This ratio was used in some cases to figure approximate trail mileage.

You will want to take the book with you so that you can use the map if you are unfamiliar with the property. A **P** designates the parking area found at the entrance to each site. Each map shows north to orient you, and we have included an approximate scale in either feet or miles. A heavy dashed line indicates the route described in the text, and the lighter dashed line indicates other trails in the area.

If you are walking with children, see the recommended walks found later in this introduction.

Conditions of trails do change from time to time, and we would appreciate hearing about any changes you find. Address them to Appalachian Mountain Club Books, 5 Joy Street, Boston, MA 02108.

Middlesex and Worcester Counties

Groton Place and Sabine Woods
Groton
200 acres

- **2.5 miles**
- **1.5 hours**
- **easy**

Groton Place and Sabine Woods are two little-known properties situated along the eastern side of the **Nashua River** in Groton. They cover a total of 200 acres of forest and fields and are managed by the New England Forestry Foundation. Some **massive white pines** grow here, as well as rhododendron, azaleas, oaks, maples, and birch. Adjacent to the properties is a strip of land owned by the Groton Conservation Trust, and together the three tracts protect over 1,800 feet of river frontage.

The walk through the properties is a relatively easy two-and-a-half-mile outing forming a large circular route. The highlight of the walk is the path along the Nashua River, which is lined by old-growth pines.

Groton Place & Sabine Woods

Route 225

P

field

rhododendrons
mtn. laurel

N

1000 feet

Sabine Woods sign

mixed
woodlands

Nashua River

large
pines

stream

Farmers Row Rd.

ball
field

hockey
arena

pool

ball
field

Groton
School

From the parking area near the river, enter the property through the large metal gate. (When leaving your
car unattended, always lock any valuables out of sight in

the trunk.) You will cross a narrow cove and enter a field where an old stone horse trough rests directly ahead. Bear left on the trail leading into the woods. The trail forks again in about 100 feet at a large stand of **rhododendron** bushes. Bear to the left again. White pines are the dominant tree here along with a scattering of oaks. The trail is fairly level and makes a great path for cross-country skiing. Horseback riders also enjoy the flat terrain, and it's quite likely you will see riders on the weekend. Soon an old stone wall parallels the trail on the left. About 15 minutes into the walk (stay on the main trail) you will pass a sign for Sabine Woods, erected for people coming down the trail the other way.

After walking another 10 minutes you will pass a ball field on your left. This is part of the sprawling campus of the Groton School. At the next intersection in a grassy area, turn right to continue your loop. You will soon reenter the woods. There is a greater variety of trees here, with oak, maple, pine, and a scattering of white birch. Look for cottontails, which are active year-round, particularly at night and early morning when they emerge from their concealed resting places to feed. They will eat all kinds of green vegetation including bark, twigs, buds, and grass. The trail passes over a small stream that flows north.

From the ball field, proceed down this trail for about 20 minutes until you reach a boathouse on the banks of the Nashua River. The river is quite a success story. In the 1960s it was considered one of the most polluted rivers in the country. Since that time, cleanup efforts have restored much of the river to a Class B rating (fishable/swimmable), and a large portion of its banks are now protected. It is one of the few north-flowing rivers in Massachusetts and drains more than 530 square miles. The watershed includes three main tributaries: the Squannacook, the Stillwater, and the Nissitissit. Groton Place and Sabine Woods are part of a larger greenway connecting open space along the Nashua River.

At the boathouse, take the trail that follows the river's flow northward. The enormous white pines that line the trail were once sought after as timber for ships' masts. In fact, the British Admiralty, through a king's decree in 1688, reserved all pines with trunk diameters of 24 inches or greater for the British navy. A broad arrow was stamped on the tree, signifying that these were crown property—a long-standing source of irritation to the colonists who worked the land.

Pines are sun-loving trees and when New England agriculture began to decline in the late nineteenth century, pines reclaimed the abandoned fields. In just a few years a thick stand of pines would dominate a field. In the understory, shade-tolerant hardwood saplings eventually appeared, and when the pines were logged or died of old age, the hardwoods took over.

The riverside trail you are walking has good views of the water, and it's possible to see wading birds such as great blue heron standing in the river or flying just above the water's surface. **Great blue heron** have wingspans of 70 inches and fly with necks folded. They are often seen standing motionless at the edge of the river watching for fish or frogs. **Green heron** are also seen here. They can be identified by the green-gray coloring of their back and wings, with chestnut-colored head and neck. They are considerably smaller than the great blue heron, and they

A great blue heron pauses from fishing.

have a comparatively shorter neck. Mammals such as raccoons, deer, fox, and weasels are active along the banks of the river. You probably have your best chance of spotting wildlife by walking the trail at dawn.

After walking along the path for 15 minutes you will reach an area where **hemlock** and **spruce** are mixed with the pines. Stay straight and do not turn on the small path entering on the right. A cement circular bench overlooking the water makes a good resting spot. (Notice the interesting statue of a resting dog next to the bench. The owner of this former estate, Mr. Frederick Dumaine, was a fox hunter and dog lover. The ashes of Mr. Dumaine are under the millstone next to the bench, and his favorite horse is buried nearby. The statue of the dog is said to be guarding this final resting place.) Just a hundred feet beyond this point is another bench—this one is situated in a field by the river so it usually receives full sunlight. It's also a good place to stop for a snack and watch for birds, such as bluebirds, that prefer the open areas rather than the forest.

To return to your car, simply walk away from the river, opposite the second set of benches, and follow the trail right through the grass. In five minutes you will be at the horse trough and bridge over the cove near the metal entrance gate where you parked. (If it's springtime, be sure to take a few moments to walk back up the trail to its first split where rhododendrons grow, as marked on the map. By staying to the right at the fork instead of going left as directed earlier, you make a short loop back toward the benches by the river.)

Getting There

From Route 495, take Exit 31 (Route 119/Groton) and follow Route 119 west 7.1 miles into Groton center. Bear left onto Route 225 west and follow for 0.7 mile. Route 225 will turn to the right. Follow it for another 0.7 mile. The turnoff for parking is just before the bridge over the river on the left. A brick and iron gate marks the entrance to the property.

Open year-round, seven days a week, no admission fee, no rest rooms.

—M.T.

Flat Rock Wildlife Sanctuary
Fitchburg
340 acres

- **1.5 miles**
- **1 hour**
- **medium**
- **great for children**

Walking the trails of Flat Rock Wildlife Sanctuary, it seems as though you are miles from civilization, instead of a few minutes from downtown Fitchburg. Beech, hemlock, and birch form a canopy above mountain laurel. Below these is a rich diversity of ferns, moss, and ground cover such as winterberry and partridgeberry. The trail system is quite extensive with multiple entry points to this 340-acre sanctuary managed by the Massachusetts Audubon Society (MAS). This walk covers the westernmost portion of the property near the main entrance on Ashburnham Hill Road.

On my first trip to Flat Rock, I had the pleasure of walking the property with Gail Howe, a Massachusetts Audubon Society naturalist. Gail's keen eye for nature's subtleties gave me a perspective of the sanctuary I would have missed had I gone alone. We also had the good fortune of walking in mid-October under a crystal blue sky that highlighted the brilliant foliage.

Flat Rock Wildlife Sanctuary

Ashburnham Hill Rd.

N

500 feet

barn

P

sphagnum

power line

pasture with
transition

Bald Top

We started our trip by following the trail that begins adjacent to the little barn by the parking area (two large posts mark the beginning of the trail). It's an uphill climb, passing old stone walls and **witch hazel,** which has small yellow flowers blooming in the fall. The flowers appear in clusters of two or three in the axils of the leaves. A furry woody seed capsule of the previous season appears with the flowers, and when this capsule splits it ejects the seed, propelling it for many yards. Witch hazel is a tall shrub (usually about 10 feet) with dull, deep olive green leaves from two to six inches long. In the autumn when the flowers begin to open, the leaves turn a spotted, dull gold. A little higher up on the trail, the smooth gray trunks of beech trees dominate the woodlands. In autumn their yellow-bronze leaves flutter in the breeze. Gail pointed out a multitude of chipmunk holes (about one and a half inches in diameter) along the side of the trail, and we saw quite a few busily gathering acorns.

Gail also identified a sign of the **pileated woodpecker**—a pile of chips at the base of a dead tree where it had chiseled into the soft wood in search of wood-boring insects such as carpenter ants. Nearby, we saw the tracks of white-tailed deer that had also used this trail, probably to feed on the popple trees near the summit. (Popple and poplar are names given to the American aspen.) Deer tracks can be identified by a heart-shaped footprint with a ridge in the center. The animal is traveling in the direction the narrow end is pointed. Deer are quite abundant in Massachusetts now, but it was not always so: in Thoreau's essay *The Natural History of Massachusetts,* written in 1842, I was surprised by his lament that "the bear, wolf, lynx, wildcat, deer, beaver and marten have disappeared. . . ."

If you look closely at the surrounding woods, it's possible to see the signs of a fire that burned much of the underbrush in 1992. You will also see staghorn sumac, so named because the stems feel like the velvet antlers on a deer during the summer months while the antlers are still growing. In late summer, the sumac's red fruit brightens the margins of the deeper woods, and in the fall the leaves turn a rich crimson. The sumac usually grows only to 10 or 12 feet but occasionally reaches heights up to 45 feet. It grows in large clumps in old pastures and open areas but never in deep, shaded woods. Sumac leaves are large (12 to 24 inches) and are made up of 11 to 31 toothed leaflets.

By staying on the main trail, you will first pass a trail branching off to the right after 10 minutes; continue straight and in 5 minutes you'll reach a vista that overlooks a meadow and the hills to the southwest. This is a nice spot to rest in the sun, before completing a small loop that takes you back to the main trail. Head back down the hill a short distance (past the start of the loop), and turn onto the first path to the left. On this trail, Gail pointed out clubmoss, growing like miniature pine trees, and the sprouts of American chestnut coming out of an old stump. Unfortunately, chestnut blight, a disease introduced to this country from Asia early in this century, kills the chestnut before the sprouts have a chance to mature. Gail observed that the tree "perseveres, keeps trying to come back." Scientists are working hard to conquer chestnut blight; perhaps someday the stately chestnuts will once again fill the New England woods.

This side trail is rather narrow and rocky, with glacial erratics scattered about and mountain laurel growing in the shallow soil beneath the woods of beech. About 10 minutes down this path, be on the lookout for a tiny patch of **sphagnum** in a moist area to the left of the trail. (Feel how spongy the sphagnum is—because of its ability to absorb water, Native Americans used it for diapers.) Bogs form in wet places, such as old glacial lakes created when blocks of ice deposited by the glaciers melted. Peat often accumulates to considerable depths. Because peat is deficient in many minerals needed for plant growth, only a few specialized species such as sphagnum mosses can grow in the extremely acidic, nutrient-poor soil.

After walking a few more minutes, you will see a trail on the left with blue paint dots on trees, indicating this trail leads away from the parking area (yellow dots signify that you are going toward the parking area). Take this trail to the left to extend your walk. It is referred to as the Link Trail and heads to the east. Within 10 minutes

Enjoying the sun and vista at Flat Rock.

you will pass beneath power lines and then through land that is in transition from pasture to forest. Small white pines, oaks, and blueberry are scattered about. The small birch trees you see here are gray birch, which rarely grow beyond 30 feet tall and often occur in clumps. Gray birch typically grows in poor soil of old fields or burned-out areas. Although it is of little value as lumber, the seeds and buds are eaten by ruffed grouse and songbirds.

Ahead is a bald area of granite rock ledge that makes a nice sunny spot to picnic. To return to the parking area simply retrace your steps back on the Link Trail, and then bear left at its end for a short walk to your car.

(Intrepid explorers may want to continue toward the east from the bald area, but the trails can be a bit confusing. Gail told me she once found a huge pellet from an owl at the base of a large pine just east of the bald. The pellet had the entire skull of a squirrel in it!)

Getting There (main entrance)

From Fitchburg center at the intersection of Routes 2A, 13, and 31, follow Route 2A west to West Street, and take the second right onto Ashburnham Hill Road. Sanctuary entrance is 1.0 mile on the right.

Open year-round, Tuesday–Sunday (closed on Monday except on major holidays), admission fee (MAS members free), no rest rooms.

—M.T.

Lincoln Woods

Leominster

68 acres

8/30/98

- **1 mile**
- **30 minutes**
- **easy**
- **great for children**

Just one mile beyond the center of Leominster, Lincoln Woods features an esker (a glacial ridge) and vernal pools that attract wildlife. The walk in this Massachusetts Audubon property is an easy one and is recommended for young children.

Begin by following the trail behind the signboard at the parking area. The woods are comprised of white pine, oak, and maple, with Canada mayflower growing in abundance among the pine needles on the forest floor. At the first split in the trail, about 150 feet from the signboard and near an activities building on the right, take the path to the right that leads into a meadow.

A stone wall runs along the edge of the meadow where garter snakes, black racers, and other snakes sometimes sun themselves. Garter snakes can be identified by the stripes running down either side of their body and a pale yellow or orange stripe running down the center of their backs. Black racers are somewhat larger and are usually a black or slate gray color.

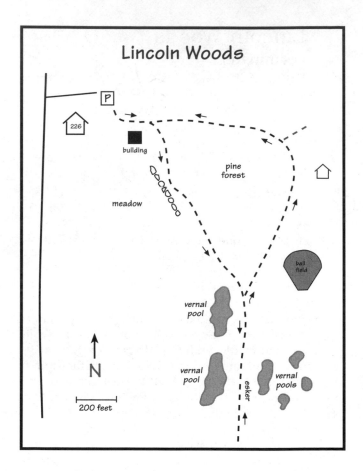

Lincoln Woods

Other wildlife here includes deer, opossum, fox, raccoon, and a wide assortment of birds, including the pileated woodpecker. Pileated woodpeckers, uncommon in Massachusetts, are large birds, 15 inches from head to tail. They use sharply pointed bills to dig into trees to get at wood-boring insects. While "drumming" into the tree the woodpecker steadies itself with its stiff tail. It can be identified by its black back and brilliant red pointed crest on the head.

After the trail crosses the meadow, it reenters the pine forest and soon passes by the first vernal pool on the right. A vernal pool is temporary, filling with water in the spring and fall but usually drying in the summer. Because fish are absent from such pools, amphibians can breed here with less threat of being eaten. These unique pools are used by wood frogs and various salamanders as breeding sites; invertebrates such as fairy shrimp spend their entire lives here. Bring along a magnifying glass so children can explore the vernal pools with you.

Blue-spotted salamanders, an endangered species classified as of "special concern," live in forests that have vernal pools. During the breeding season in spring, they lay their eggs at the bottom of vernal pools. During the rest of the year this amphibian lives entirely underground, burrowing beneath the leaf litter of the woods. They can be identified by the sky blue spots on their sides and should not be disturbed if seen.

As you walk the trail, note that you are climbing a ridge of land separating the hollows on either side. This ridge, running north-south, is an esker formed by the glaciers. Eskers are comprised of gravel deposited by a meltwater stream as it flowed through a tunnel under the ice that covered New England from 20,000 to 10,000 years ago. In some places here at Lincoln Woods, the esker is quite high and narrow.

Trails pass old stone walls leading into Lincoln Woods.

Follow the trail to the south as it climbs the esker. More vernal pools lie to the right and left. An old stone wall parallels the trail on the left, indicating that the land here was once cleared for pasture.

The trail ends at the southern section of the property. Retrace your steps back past the vernal pools, then bear right at the fork in the trail to make a loop of the woods. You will pass a ball field and private home on right. The total walk is only about a mile and is on fairly level terrain.

Getting There

Take the Leominster-Route 12 exit (Exit 31) off Route 2. Follow Route 12 south 1.9 miles to Union Street on the right. (You will have passed Leominster center.) Go right on Union Street for 0.6 mile and look for the Audubon sign on the left. There is a small entrance road just to the left of the caretaker's house (226 Union Street). Follow this road to a small parking lot.

Open year-round, closed Mondays except for major holidays, admission fee (free for MAS members), no rest rooms.

—M.T.

Wachusett Mountain State Reservation
Princeton
2,050 Acres

- **1.5 miles**
- **1 hour, 15 minutes if you descend via the Pine Hill Trail**
- **moderate/difficult**
- **great for older children**

Thoreau called it "the blue wall," and the Native Americans called it Wachusett, meaning "by the great hill." Both are apt descriptions. Seen from a distance, Wachusett does look like a blue wall standing alone in the lowlands, and it is a large and great hill for this area of Massachusetts, rising to 2,006 feet. The sprawling reservation that covers the mountain and the surrounding forest is one of our better state parks, with a great number of well-marked trails, excellent wildlife habitat, and some super views. The walk to the top is not especially difficult, and, with a couple of rests, most people should have little trouble.

The relatively short walk to the summit described here is just one of several ways to reach the top, and the reservation is worthy of many visits. At the visitor center you can obtain a free map that shows all the trails, including those on the Westminster side of the moun-

Wachusett Mountain State Reservation

Summit Road

N

1000 feet

Harrington Trail

View to
Mt. Monadnock

View to
Boston

Jack Frost Trail

Mtn. House Trail

Echo Lake

Jack Frost Trail

High Meadow

Mtn. House Trail

Loop Trail

Summit Road

Echo Lake Road

P

Bicentennial Trail

Visitor Center

Mountain Rd.

P

tain. The Westminster area includes "Balance Rock," left behind by retreating glaciers; streams; and an old-growth red oak forest. In fact, it's worth taking a circular drive around the mountain to see the beautiful countryside. And for anyone who is mobility impaired, the access road to the summit is open for driving during warm-weather months.

Begin your walk at the reservation's main parking lot and follow the Bicentennial Trail. (Blue triangular blazes mark all the trails.) It's only a few minutes to a sign for the Loop Trail, where you should turn right and begin the ascent of the mountain. This trail has plenty of rocks, so keep an eye on the ground to see where to plant your next step. Be sure to stop and admire the oak woods and scan the hills ahead for wildlife such as grouse, fox, or deer.

Soon a view opens up on the left. This is a good place to pause and catch your breath. The scene is to the east, and on a clear day you can see the Boston skyline in the distance. Notice that the land stretching toward Boston is relatively flat. Wachusett Mountain is a **monadnock,** a mountain that rises high and virtually alone above the flat plateau. Formed more than 100 million years ago, the mountain is composed of once molten granite. Over the course of millions of years the mountain has been worn down by wind, water, and glacial erosion. It is estimated that at one time Wachusett was thousands of feet taller, perhaps as high as 23,000 feet above sea level. Other mountains made of softer rock than granite once surrounded Wachusett, but they were completely leveled by erosion.

The surrounding woods are primarily comprised of oaks, and I've observed many woodpecker holes in the dead wood, possibly from pileated woodpeckers. The pileated woodpecker is an elusive bird, but because of its large size (about as big as a crow) you might get lucky and spot one. Listen for its drumming, which begins loud, then slows, and finally is softer before ending. The birds are best identified by the distinctive red crest and solid black back.

As you climb the trail, try to find your rhythm as you pick your way over the rocks. Mountain hikes can be incredibly relaxing when you focus solely on the hike and forget the outside world. In about 20 minutes you will arrive at the junction with the Mountain House Trail. Turn right and head north toward the summit.

Once I hiked up Wachusett in November, and this area of the mountain was especially beautiful. The bare trees stood out boldly against the granite rocks and the crystal blue southwestern sky. A scattering of beech trees showed off their smooth gray trunks, and a few yellow leaves clung tenaciously to lower branches. Another advantage of hiking here in November is that the access road to the summit is closed, so you may have the summit to yourself. As with any fall hike, be sure to wear something red or orange during hunting season.

The open mountaintop appears in another 20-minute walk, and you are rewarded with views in all directions. To the northwest you can see the outline of Mt. Monadnock and in the distance the smooth rolling shape of Vermont's Green Mountains. On clear days, Mt. Tom can be seen far to the west along the Connecticut River valley.

Thoreau camped on Wachusett's summit, writing, "It was thrilling to hear the wind roar over the rocks." When he awakened he wrote of the vista as dawn reached its prime: "We enjoyed the view of a distinct horizon line, and could fancy ourselves at sea, and the distant hills the waves in the horizon, as seen from the deck of a vessel." Later in the 1800s a summit house was built on the mountain, signaling the beginning of recreation on Wachusett. The hotel was three stories tall and attracted visitors from Boston and New York. Princeton had 12 hotels and was a thriving tourist town for visitors to escape the heat and hustle of the city and enjoy the clean mountain air.

The view of the surrounding lowlands from the summit in those days would have been far different than it is today. Instead of the green canopy of trees, the landscape was one of fields and pasture. Agriculture was king in Massachusetts until the late 1800s, when farmers were drawn west, away from its stony fields. First white pine, gray birch, sumac, and aspen reclaimed a field, followed by oak, beech, and hemlock. The forest, still changing today, will reach the climax stage when hickory, hemlock, sugar maple, oak, and beech dominate.

September is a wonderful time to visit Wachusett because that is when the hawk migration is in full force. Thousands of broad-winged and lesser numbers of sharp-shinned hawks ride the thermals above the ridges. Sometimes other species such as eagles and turkey vultures pass through. The migration is a thrilling sight if you hit it right. However, be warned that in mid-September you won't have the mountaintop to yourself, as many others will be there to enjoy the annual event.

There are many different routes you can take to descend the mountain. You might try the Jack Frost Trail, which has stands of hemlock and mountain laurel in its

A hawk surveys surrounding terrain from its perch.

lower reaches. The Jack Frost Trail connects to the High Meadow Trail, and you can walk southwest to see Echo Lake before heading back to the parking area via the Bicentennial Trail. Echo Lake is a small, shallow lake with a picnic table and stone fireplace at its eastern end. High Meadow is an area of transition where the once open field is being reclaimed by the forest, now covered with birch, sumac, and blackberry bushes. It affords a partial view to the southeast.

The quickest way off the summit is to descend via the Pine Hill Trail, but this route should be taken only in dry weather because it is very steep and much of the trail is exposed bedrock. The trail has some great views to the east. Hemlocks and white birch line the trail and, in the springtime, mayflowers bloom. Descending on this trail only takes about 15 minutes.

Be sure to stop in at the visitor center—the displays are excellent.

Getting There

From Route 2 take Exit 25, Route 140 south, and go south on Route 140 for 2.6 miles. Turn right at the State Park sign and follow Mile Hill Road, which soon turns into Mountain Road. Parking is 1.8 miles from Route 140.

No admission fee; rest rooms in visitor center; open seven days a week, year-round.

—M.T.

Broad Meadow Brook Wildlife Sanctuary
Worcester
272 acres

- **2.5 miles**
- **1.5 hours**
- **easy**
- **great for children**

Broad Meadow Brook Wildlife Sanctuary is like an oasis of green in the urbanized area around Worcester. It acts as a resting place for many migratory birds and is home to a surprising amount of wildlife such as mink, deer, raccoon, red fox, rabbit, opossum, and woodchuck. The 272-acre property, with marsh, brooks, and woods, is the largest urban wildlife sanctuary in New England.

The walk begins by following the Holdridge Trail around to the left of the visitor center and into a woods of maple, quaking aspen, ash, and oak. About five minutes into the walk, you come to a boardwalk at marker number 1 and turn left. (Markers are placed at all trail intersections.) This is the Cutover Trail, which leads past a tiny frog pond on your left. On my last visit, with my family in late September, we spotted two frogs and a large **snake** beneath the cattails. We waited for the snake to show more of itself so we could try to identify it, but it was content to lie motionless, with just its head sticking out of the water.

Broad Meadow Brook Wildlife Sanctuary

power lines

Massasoit Road

brook

N

400 feet

Outer Loop West Trail

Outer Loop East Trail

Cattail Marsh

Visitor Center

P

brook

Holdridge Trail

power lines

Magic Loop Trail

Broad Meadow Brook

Cutover Trail

Frog Pond

glacial erratic

Buttonbush Pond

Sprague Trail

The trail soon passes by some private homes on the left, and in five minutes you will have reached the end of the Cutover Trail. On your right will be the Sprague Trail, a wide, flat path that borders an old stone wall. It is an excellent place for birding because of its openness. The sanctuary is home to some 60 species of **birds** that breed on the property, such as ruffed grouse, red-tailed hawk, northern flicker, and hairy woodpecker. Smaller birds such as eastern wood-pewee, common yellowthroats, bluebirds, and warblers are often present. Wood ducks, great horned owls, eastern screech owls, and wild turkeys also have been observed.

About an eighth of a mile down the Sprague Trail, Broad Meadow Brook passes under the trail, flowing south toward the Blackstone River. The granite slab that serves as a bridge over the brook is a perfect place to sit and rest. Look down into the pool below the small waterfall for crayfish and minnows. Some lucky explorers have seen muskrat and raccoon at this spot. **Mink** are also known to frequent this pool. Adult males can grow as long as 35 inches including their tail, yet the weight of a mink that size would be only about two and a half pounds. They are crafty hunters that prey primarily on small rodents but will also take birds, snakes, frogs, crayfish, and even muskrat.

On the edge of the brook you might notice a slender plant two to four feet tall with bright red flowers blooming during late summer. This is the **cardinal flower,** which grows in wet places throughout New England. You may also notice skunk cabbage and other plants that prefer swampy areas. While identifying plant life, be sure to look closely at the muddy banks along the stream—chances are you will find the tracks of raccoons that make nocturnal visits to pools such as this and use their sensitive forefeet, with humanlike fingers, to feel for frogs, mussels, and crayfish. The tracks are relatively easy to distinguish from other animals because the developed "toes" and "fingers" make the tracks look similar to a child's handprint.

The Sprague Trail narrows after crossing the stream and rises through a woodland where ferns grow alongside the path, and oaks become the dominant tree. Pass marker number 3 and the Magic Loop Trail branching to the right. Continue on for about five more minutes of walking to marker number 4. Bear right here, and you will pass tiny **Buttonbush Pond** on the left, home to spotted turtles and spotted salamanders. The buttonbush has distinctive ball-like white-colored flowers on stems that range from 3 to 10 feet tall. Because the vegetation is thick here, the best time to see the turtles is in the early spring, before the vegetation obscures your view. Look for turtles basking in the sun on a log.

Just beyond Buttonbush Pond, there is a **glacial erratic** on the right that kids will enjoy climbing. Large boulders such as this are called erratics because during the Ice Age glaciers carried them many miles and deposited them in areas of different bedrock. The glacier that advanced on New England carved valleys where none had previously existed, scoured existing river valleys, and plucked stones off ledges and ground them before depositing when the ice began to melt 10,000 to 15,000 years ago. Many erratics appear in unusual locations, often balanced high on a hilltop.

Not far from the boulder is marker number 5, where you should bear left. This is the Outer Loop West Trail, which leads toward the western perimeter of the property. About five minutes down this trail, after crossing a brook, reach marker number 6. Here either bear right and stay on the Outer Loop West Trail, which goes northward through the woods, or walk beneath the adjacent power lines and follow them to the right.

I prefer the power line trail, because it is a good

Hikers at Broad Meadow pause for a streamside rest.

place to spot **butterflies** such as monarchs and black swallowtails. Beneath the sunny opening of the power lines grow many wildflowers, such as Queen Anne's lace, asters, and goldenrod. After walking about 10 or 15 minutes under the power lines, look for a footpath on the right that leads back into the woods of the sanctuary. (Look for this path just before the power line service road swings to the left side of the power lines.) The Outer Loop West Trail will also enter from the right.

Walk through a birch and poplar grove, pass marker number 9, and within a couple minutes reach marker number 8 where you should bear slightly to the right. The Outer Loop East Trail hugs a ridge, and to the left is a low-lying area where water collects. It is a good 15-minute walk on this trail, which allows your mind to roam while your legs carry you on automatic pilot.

When you reach marker number 7, bear left onto the Holdridge Trail, which leads back toward the parking area. There are some wonderful old oak trees that spread their canopies above this trail. Just stay straight and you will return to the visitor center. Plan on spending about an hour and a half for this walk, a bit longer if you are with children. Chances are, kids will want to revisit the frog pond to look for more snakes, frogs, and tadpoles.

Getting There

From the Massachusetts Turnpike, take the Millbury exit (Exit 11) and turn left off the ramp onto Route 122 heading north. Follow Route 122 for 0.7 mile and then go left on Route 20 west. Proceed 0.9 mile and then turn right on Massasoit Road at the first traffic light. The sanctuary is 0.5 mile ahead on the left.

From Route 290 west, take Exit 13/Vernon Street and turn left (if on Route 290 east take Exit 13 and turn right). Proceed up Vernon Street and take the left fork onto Winthrop Street. Follow Winthrop Street past Providence Street and St. Vincent's Hospital, where it becomes Heywood Street. Go straight on Heywood to the bottom of the hill, and turn right onto Massasoit Road. The sanctuary is 1.4 miles ahead on the right.

Open Tuesday through Sunday, dawn to dusk. Admission fee for nonmembers of Massachusetts Audubon; free to the residents of Worcester Tuesday through Friday. Visitor center and rest room open 9:00 A.M. to 4:00 P.M.

—M.T.

Purgatory Chasm
State Reservation

Sutton

960 acres   *10/23/99*

w/ Tim, Buffy
and Jamie .

- 0.5 mile
- 30 minutes
- medium
- great for children

A good name always piques my curiosity and Purgatory Chasm certainly has one. Sometimes the name builds you up for a big letdown when you actually visit the place, but that's not the case here. The chasm, with its sheer rock walls towering 70 feet above the trail, is a dramatic place to explore.

From the parking area, follow the sign to the chasm and begin your descent into the base of the crevice. You must pick your way around **massive boulders,** and children should be accompanied by an adult. Be sure to wear rubber-soled shoes or hiking boots. (Because the footing can be treacherous during periods of snow and ice, the chasm is usually closed December through March.) The jumble of rocks forms a series of small dark caves, crevices, and jagged outcrops, adding to the mysterious, other-worldly feeling.

One can't help but wonder how the chasm was formed. Did the earth open during an earthquake? Did

Purgatory Chasm

ranger station

P

Purgatory Road

P

P

ball field

N

300 feet

Charley's Loop Trail

Chasm

The Corn Crib

Fat Man's Misery

East Rim

Chasm Loop Trail

The Coffin

Charley's Loop Trail

Charley's Loop Trail

the glaciers split the bedrock? Park Ranger Dave Podles told me the most likely theory: the chasm was formed when a giant glacial lake released its water and ice, which tore through the rock and opened the crevice. Later, freezing and thawing made the sides split and rocks tumbled to the bottom.

It takes about 10 minutes to reach the base of the chasm, where a few trees somehow manage to grow. A couple of **old-growth hemlock** trees are truly spectacular. Towering overhead, their crowns extend beyond the edge of the cliff above. They are perhaps 300 years old. It was impractical for eighteenth- and nineteenth-century loggers to haul them out of here, and thus they were spared the fate of so many other large ancient New England trees. Take a moment to examine the roots of the trees, which snake around the boulders, searching for a bit of dirt to sink into. A scattering of ferns and lichens is about the only other vegetation that can grow in the shadows of the chasm.

It seems remarkable to me that the floor of the chasm stays dry because it looks like a river gorge without the water. Perhaps that's why it's been called New England's Grand Canyon. This canyon is just one-fourth-mile long, though, and soon you leave the granite cliffs behind. Mixed with the granite are small sections of quartz, mica, and gneiss.

When you reach the end of the chasm, turn left and walk back toward the parking area via the eastern rim on the Chasm Loop Trail. There are a few overlooks that allow a view down into the chasm, but be sure to exercise caution. Some of the **unique geological formations** in the rim have been named. Fat Man's Misery is a nar-

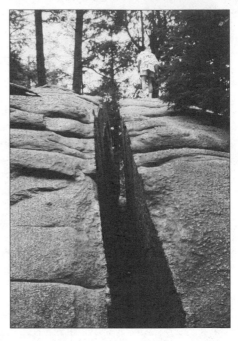

Fat Man's Misery.

row crack in the rock—big enough for a thin person to walk through but trouble for someone with a few extra pounds. On my visits, I opt not to test the dark alley.

"The Coffin" and "The Corn Crib" were originally called the devil's coffin and devil's corncrib by the Puritans, who likened the chasm to a descent toward Hades. The coffin has a rock in the shape of a coffin, and the corncrib looks like an early settler's corncrib.

The walk along the rim is relatively easy compared to the climb down into the chasm. The whole loop only takes about half an hour, and you may want to explore some of the less frequented nearby trails through woods of oak, white pine, and hemlock. Charley's Loop Trail begins at the pavilion near the parking area and heads in a southerly direction for half a mile until a T junction, where you should turn right. Follow the trail for about a quarter of a mile and then take the next right, which will bring you to the far end of the chasm. From here you can return to the parking lot by going through the chasm or walking either rim trail.

(Photography in the chasm can be a real challenge. One thing I've learned from repeat visits is that to better capture the scale of the boulders, trees, and cliffs, it's best to have people in the shot. Besides adding a sense of dimension, a person hiking through the chasm gives the photo needed contrast against the dark gray, shadowy rocks.)

Climbing the chasm walls is strictly prohibited without a permit. Serious injuries have occurred here. Wear rubber-soled shoes or hiking books as the trails are slippery, and stay away from the edges of the chasm.

Getting There

Purgatory Chasm is located just off Route 146 in Sutton. (Route 146 runs from the Worcester area southward to Uxbridge on the Rhode Island border.) Exit Route 146 at the Purgatory Road Sutton exit. Signs will direct you to the reservation, about a half mile west on Purgatory Road.

Closed during periods of snow and ice, otherwise open seven days a week, no admission fee, rest rooms.

—M.T.

Blackstone River and Canal Heritage State Park
Northbridge/Uxbridge
1,005 acres

- **3 miles**
- **1.5 hours**
- **medium**

When William Blackstone, the first European settler of Shawmut Peninsula (now Boston), decided he needed a little more elbow room, he went westward, settling along the river that now bears his name. His solitude was short-lived as other settlers followed him, cutting the virgin timber to farm the rolling hills and erecting mills along the river.

Today, one can get a sense of how this landscape must have looked when Blackstone first arrived by taking a walk to the top of King Philip's Rock. A **panoramic view** to the south encompasses the river, the wooded hills, and almost no signs of mankind.

To reach this hilltop, begin your walk by following the King Philip Trail adjacent to the office of the Department of Environmental Management on East Hartford Avenue. The gravel trail leads northward through a field where bluebird boxes have been erected. About a hundred yards from the start, the trail turns to the right (fol-

Blackstone River & Canal Heritage State Park

King Philip's Rock Overlook

red pine

King Philip Trail

Rice City Pond

▲ Goat Hill

field

D.E.M. Headquarters

P

East Hartford Ave.

stone arch bridges

Oak St.

towpath

P

N

1000 feet

low the blue markers) and enters a forest of white pines and oaks.

On your left is **Rice City Pond,** an impoundment on the Blackstone River. The pond, wetlands, and woods around it are home to raccoon, white-tailed deer, red fox, partridge, quail, turtles, and snakes. Herons, ospreys, and hawks visit the pond, and once, a rare Eurasian widgeon was seen. (Canoeists enjoy exploring the quiet, placid waters. You may want to make a day trip to the park, canoeing half the day and taking this walk the other half.)

Follow the trail through an old gravel pit and bear left at the fork on the opposite side. A couple of minutes farther on you come to an opening that overlooks the pond. If you look to the right you can see King Philip's Rock along the hillside.

Next, the trail hugs a boulder-strewn slope, where you must pick your way among the rocks and exposed roots. Notice the smooth gray trunks of small beech trees that begin to appear. Also seen are sections of stone walls, indicating that this land was once cleared for pasture or crops.

About 30 minutes from the start of your hike the trail forks; follow the blue markers to the left, passing over a small stream and through a plantation of **red pine.** A few minutes later you are near the base of King Philip's Rock, at a four-way intersection. Take the second trail to your left that leads around the sheer rock ledges toward the direction of Rice City Pond. (You can also reach the summit by following the blue markers to the right.)

The trail swings around to the left and then makes a steep climb to the top of the hill. The summit makes a

Walking trail on the original tow path adjacent to the Blackstone Canal.

great place to picnic or simply relax and enjoy the view of the meandering river and pond below. In the spring, I enjoy seeing the pattern of dark green pines mix with the lighter colored new growth of deciduous trees. Autumn brings the orange-brown of oaks and the reds of swamp maples. Often, cool breezes sweep over the hill, refreshing after the 40-minute walk through the lowlands.

King Philip's Rock was named for the Wampanoag leader Metacom, whom the English called Philip. It was Metacom who led the 1675–76 uprising of a number of regional tribes against the settlers pushing westward from coastal areas. Like so many rocky bluffs in Massachusetts, local legend has it that this spot was one of the places where Philip and his followers camped during King Philip's War. While we may never know where Philip actually set foot, the hilltop offers the best view of the Blackstone River, whose historic tale is as interesting as its natural one.

Originating in Worcester, the Blackstone drains an area of 640 square miles during its south-southeastward course to Rhode Island's Narragansett Bay. Along the way there are a number of historic points of interest, most involving the mills and the **canal** that connected Worcester to Providence.

The Slater Mill (1793), located by the river in Pawtucket, Rhode Island, was America's first mechanized textile mill. More mills quickly followed, and the explosion of manufacturing along the banks of the river led to the area being labeled as the "Birthplace of the American Industrial Revolution." Mill villages with holding ponds, dams, old brick factories, and simple mill housing are found all along the river.

In 1824, construction of the canal began. Using shovels, axes, picks, wheelbarrows, and ox carts, laborers (mostly immigrants from Ireland who were paid $12 a month) dug the 45-mile canal. Canal owners installed expensive granite locks rather than the more economical wooden locks and planted trees along both sides of the canal for erosion control. But their investment did not reap long-term profits. In 1848, the completion of the Providence and Worcester Railroad marked the beginning of the end for the canal.

After you follow the original trail back off the hill and retrace your path to the parking area, take the time to walk the old towpath along the canal. My favorite spot is near the new River Bend Farm Visitor Center on Oak Street. The visitor center features exhibits depicting the history of the Blackstone River valley. From the parking lot at River Bend Farm, walk down to the canal and cross the handsome bridge to the towpath. If you walk to the right (south), the trail passes through an open area with the river on one side and the canal on the other (this trail goes all the way to Stanley Woolen Mill, about one and a half miles away). The path also follows the canal to the north, where a 10-minute walk will bring you to the beautiful falls at the stone arch bridges, and extends another two miles north to Plummers Landing.

Getting There

From the intersection of Routes 16 and 122 in Uxbridge take Route 122 north 1.3 miles to Hartford Avenue. Go right on Hartford Avenue 1.0 mile to river. For the trail to King Philip's Rock cross the river and park at the lot at the Department of Environmental Management headquarters on the left. To walk along the canal turn south on Oak Street (on the west side of the Hartford Avenue bridge over the river). After a thousand feet, a sign will welcome you to the state park.

Open year-round, seven days a week, no admission fee, no rest rooms.

—M.T.

Douglas State Forest
Douglas
4,555 acres

- **1 mile**
- **30 minutes**
- **easy**
- **great for children**

Douglas State Park has something for almost everyone: a lake for swimming, boating, and fishing; miles of forest roads for mountain biking and hiking; and an **Atlantic white cedar swamp** for nature study. You will see unique plants that grow in the cedar swamp that are not found in common marshes.

The Cedar Swamp Trail begins near the lake. From the main parking area, follow the path to the beach, then bear right past the rest rooms and small nature center to a sign that points to the trail. (In the off-season, you can park at the boat ramp adjacent to the beach.)

The trail begins as a narrow path winding through a forest of oak and maple with mountain laurel beneath. You will pass the intersection with the returning trail on your right, and you should bear left. Soon a sign points to a bird blind, located just a few feet off the Cedar Swamp Trail. The blind looks out over a slope where birdhouses and bird feeders have been erected. Look for

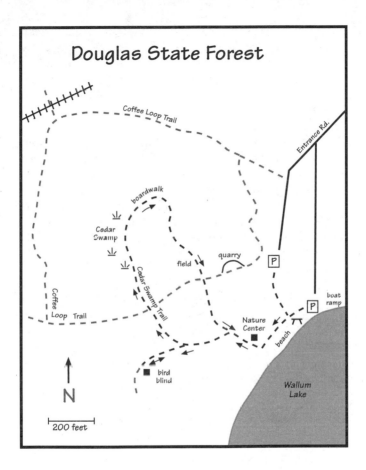

Douglas State Forest

titmice, chickadees, and blue jays at the feeders, and look for ruffed grouse on the forest floor.

Back on the Cedar Swamp Trail, the path climbs exposed granite ledges where small hemlocks grow. An interpretive sign directs your attention to **American chestnut tree sprouts.** The sprouts you see rarely grow beyond 20 feet tall before the blight, which began killing American chestnuts in 1904, enters the trees through cracks in the bark and kills them. Once common throughout the New England forest, the grand chestnut trees are no more.

Just 10 minutes into our walk, the Cedar Swamp Trail crosses the Coffee Loop Trail and descends down a hill, onto a boardwalk. Pass skunk cabbage (which Native Americans rubbed on themselves when hunting to cover their scent), cinnamon ferns, and sweet pepperbush, known for its late-summer fragrance. Skunk cabbage can be identified not only by its odor but also by its large green leaves that resemble rhubarb. It likes to have moist feet.

You are now entering the Atlantic white cedar swamp. The woods begin to feel entirely different: cooler, moister, quieter. A stand of Atlantic white cedar such as this is relatively uncommon because so many of the trees have been cut for lumber. The stand is also unusual because this is about the northernmost location for the species, with most of the New England stands being near the warmer coast. The trees grow from 40 to 50 feet in height and have scalelike, flattened green leaves.

Atlantic white cedar was popular because of its decay-resistant quality and light weight, making it perfect for fence posts, floorboards, joists, and shingles. The trees you see around you are about 70 years old and six to eight inches in diameter.

A thick expanse of sphagnum, or peat moss, covers the ground like a spongy carpet. The moss is capable of

The shores of Wallum Lake offer great picnic spots.

holding 20 times its weight in water, and Native Americans lined their babies' pants with it because of its absorbent nature. Also growing in the swamp is an insect-eating plant called the sundew. It is a small plant with rounded leaves and white or pink flowers growing just inches off the ground. Insects get trapped in the sticky fluid on its leaves and are digested by the plant.

The boardwalk ends at a rocky area where a **glacial erratic,** so named because the boulder was deposited here from far away by the retreating glacier, can be seen. Farther along the path, you come to another section of boardwalk leading through more cedars to the lower end of a field.

Approach the field quietly and be on the lookout for white-tailed deer feeding along the edge of the meadow. Red fox, ruffed grouse, and cottontail rabbits have also been seen here. Dawn and dusk are the best times to view wildlife.

Go straight through the field and follow the middle trail (which intersects the Coffee Loop Trail) to return to the **beach.** The beach is well maintained, and Wallum Lake looks like a perfect place for a dip after a walk. It is also a great area for picnicking—my favorite spot is a secluded portion of shoreline to the right (as you face the water) where three picnic tables are located by the water's edge.

For a longer walk try the Coffee Loop Trail, which makes a 2.2-mile circle of the cedar swamp.

Getting There

From the east: at the intersection of Routes 146 and 16 go west on Route 16 (passing through East Douglas and Douglas) for about 7.0 miles. At Cedar Street (1.6 miles past the Douglas town common) turn left. Signs direct you to the park entrance, 1.7 miles from your turn onto Cedar Street.

From the west: take Route 395 to the Route 16 exit (Douglas/Webster) and follow Route 16 east for 5.0 miles. Follow the signs for the park by turning right on Cedar Street.

Open year-round, seven days a week, fee during summer months, rest rooms.

—M.T.

Royalston Falls

Royalston   2/9/97

205 acres

- **3 miles**
- **1.5–2 hours**
- **easy to medium depending where you park**

One of the reasons I like Royalston Falls so much is the walk down the secluded country road to reach the property where the waterfall is located. Four-wheel-drive vehicles can drive this latter part of Falls Road to the trailhead, but the walk down the road is half the fun. Old stone walls, large hemlocks, birch, and maples line the road and are best enjoyed on foot. This way you can relish the scents, sounds, and tranquillity of the woods.

The first part of Falls Road is maintained by the town and you should drive down the road about two and a half miles to where it becomes rough and a sign says Seasonal Use. Park near the sign or at a turnoff about 100 feet past the sign. Be sure you do not block the road.

The walk down the road from the Seasonal Use sign to the Trustees' sign welcoming you to Royalston Falls takes about 25 minutes. The Royalston Falls sign is on the left just after a sharp bend in the road as it climbs a hill. A narrow trail to the falls begins here. This half-mile

Royalston Falls

The Falls

Falls

Trustees sign

Road

P

To Upper Falls
parking area
1 mile

stream

stream

Falls Brook

N

500 feet

foot trail goes over small hills of pines, hemlocks, and oaks.

These woods are home to just about every type of animal found in Massachusetts including the **fisher,** a member of the weasel family. It is a skillful predator, tracking down mice, squirrels, snowshoe hares, chipmunks, birds, and frogs. It is one of the few animals that can kill a porcupine and does so by circling the porcupine, biting its head, and wearing the creature down before moving in for the kill.

Soon you will hear the **falls** ahead. Descend a steep slope to the edge of a cliff above the falls where a railing has been erected for your safety. Falls Brook plunges about 70 feet below into a spray of mist and foam, truly a beautiful sight. The falls are inaccessible, but if you want to do a bit of bushwhacking you can follow the Falls Brook upstream along a faint path that is actually part of the Metacomet-Monadnock Trail. You can also go to the left as you face the falls and descend a slope that leads downstream into an open area about a hundred yards from the falls. It's a beautiful spot where the stream fans out into a pool framed by **ferns** and rocky outcrops.

Streamside vegetation includes cinnamon fern, a tall (three- to five-foot) plant whose fronds are covered by tufts of cinnamon brown wool in spring as well as separate brown-colored spore-producing fronds. These brown stalks wither as the season progresses, while green vegetative fronds persist. In the early spring look for skunk cabbage identified by its large purple-green shell-like spathe, which emerges from damp earth, later to be encircled by dark green cabbagelike leaves. It has a fetid odor that is especially strong if the leaves are bruised. The odor lures insects that pollinate the skunk cabbage. Its growth is so fast in the spring that the heat from its cellular respiration can actually melt snow or ice around it! Other plants you may notice are cardinal flowers, which have many brilliant red tubular flowers that bloom from July into September.

Royalston Falls tumbles over ancient rock formations.

Retrace your steps on the trail to return to Falls Road. From this point, its about a 25-minute walk back to the parking area. Because Royalston Falls is so far off the beaten path, it **receives few visitors.** The trail to the falls makes a great walk in the autumn when the mosquitoes and blackflies are gone and the hardwoods put on their annual show of color. The yellow leaves of the birches are especially beautiful, made more so by the contrast of the dark green needles of pines and hemlocks. The white birch is also known as paper birch and canoe birch because the Native Americans in northern New England used birch bark canoes.

Spring snowmelt is a spectacular time to see the falls, when the water thunders into the pool below. Blackflies are usually in full force by late April and early May, so pack bug spray. Because Royalston is at the northern border of Massachusetts, these shaded woods may still have snow cover when areas to the south and east have none. Wear hiking boots for protection and proper footing.

Getting There

From the center of Royalston take Route 68 north 1.4 miles (passing Jacobs Hill Reservation). Turn right on Falls Road and travel 3.2 miles. (Note: last 0.8 mile is not maintained by the town. If you don't have four-wheel drive, walk down this last section of roadway.)

(One of the easiest ways to get to Royalston center is to exit Route 2 onto Route 202 north. Follow for 2.4 miles and turn left onto Route 68 north and travel 8.6 miles to the center of Royalston.)

Open year-round, seven days a week, no admission fee, no rest rooms.

—M.T.

In Athol Don't take 32. Just go straight

Jacobs Hill Reservation
Royalston
135 acres   2/16/97

- **2.5 miles**
- **2 hours**
- **medium**
- **great for children**

For such a beautiful property, Jacobs Hill sure is a well-kept secret! **Spectacular views,** forested hills, a **beaver pond,** and a **waterfall** await your discovery. Best of all, the top of Jacobs Hill can be reached in an easy 15-minute walk, while more challenging terrain awaits those who want to extend their trip and explore Spirit Falls to the south. Richard O'Brien, Central Region supervisor for The Trustees of Reservations, has seen a wide array of animals here including **coyote, bobcat, porcupine, fisher, deer,** and **beaver.**

From the parking area follow the trail through woods of hemlock and beech with an understory of mountain laurel. About 200 yards down the path you will cross under a power line, and the trail resumes on the other side. (Look for highbush and lowbush blueberries in the sunny opening beneath the power line.)

Follow the yellow markers as the trail begins to climb the ridge known as Jacobs Hill. About 10 minutes from the start of your walk the trail forks—bear right.

Jacobs Hill

Route 68

Little Pond

East Branch Tully River

power lines

Long Pond

N

500 feet

Beaver pond

Spirit Falls

stream

About 3 minutes later you arrive at an intersection where you should bear left. Within a couple of minutes you will be at the edge of the ridge. Turn right to reach the scenic view lookout.

On your way to the exposed ridge top look for large woodpecker holes in a hemlock, perhaps the work of a **pileated woodpecker.** A rather uncommon bird, the pileated woodpecker is sometimes seen in this forest, its pecking noise reverberating through the woods. It is a large bird with a distinctive red head.

Within five minutes you will have reached the open area that looks out over Long Pond and the rolling hills to the west. This ridge rises 300 feet above the pond, and you can look out over the water and see the forested slopes of Tully Mountain, Mt. Grace, and other rolling hills. I love this spot, often sitting here for extended peri-

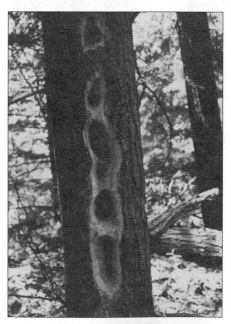

Pileated woodpecker holes open the heart of a hemlock tree on the ridge at Jacobs Hill.

ods of time with a pair of binoculars. I've seen turkey vultures and hawks ride the thermals above the pond below and sometimes they pass within 20 or 30 feet of my perch. I also like to scan the marshy area to the north, where the East Branch of the Tully River winds its way into the valley and pond. It looks like moose country, and although I've yet to see one, I think it's just a matter of time. Every year more and more moose sightings are recorded in Massachusetts.

Westerly breezes wash over Jacobs Hill, making this the perfect place to relax and enjoy quiet contemplation. When I visit I'm reminded of a quote by English writer Aldous Huxley: "My father considered a walk among the mountains as the equivalent of churchgoing." Amen.

To continue toward Spirit Falls, retrace your steps along the ridge (passing the path that heads toward the parking area) and continue straight in a southerly direction. The trail you are on is quite rocky but relatively straight, hugging the ridge top. If it's wintertime, look for the pigeon-toed tracks of the **porcupine** and its quill marks caused by the dragging tail. One of the surest ways to identify a porcupine trail is to look for signs of its browse: branches cut at 45-degree angles often litter the forest floor beneath a tree where a porcupine has been feeding. I once hiked near Jacobs Hill with expert tracker and author Paul Rezendes. He pointed out hemlock trees thoroughly stunted by browsing porcupines. A well-worn trail through the snow led from the hemlocks to an exposed rock ledge where we found numerous porcupine dens. While hiking the forest of Jacobs Hill, look up into the trees; you just might spot the dark shape of porcupines quietly feeding.

You will reach the stream that feeds Spirit Falls after about a 10- or 15-minute walk from the lookout area atop Jacobs Hill. A series of cascades lies downstream and it's a difficult climb, with no real trail to follow. For that reason I don't advise families with children to make the climb, nor would I recommend it during winter when the footing is treacherous. During the other seasons you might want to test your "mountain goat legs" and follow the stream down the hillside to watch the stream cascade over moss-covered ledges of granite. Enormous hemlocks and pines grow among the boulders here, and I enjoy photographing this special place.

To complete your loop and head back to the parking area, go back to the main trail and follow it upstream. Within a couple minutes you reach a marshy area. On my last visit there was a large beaver dam blocking the stream's progress, forming a shallow pond for the beavers. Approach this section quietly and you may spot one of nature's engineers paddling about. If you do, get ready for the loud "thwack" of its tail. This warning has caught me off guard more than once.

The trail turns back to the north here. It's about a 25-minute walk to the intersection with the trail you used to climb Jacobs Hill earlier. If you turn right here, the trail will lead you back under the power lines and to the parking lot.

About 2,000 feet east on Route 68 is a short road on the south side of the road that leads into Little Pond. The pond is becoming a bog, surrounded by black spruce, sheep laurel, leatherleaf, and tamarack. A sphagnum moss mat can be seen growing around the edge of the open water.

Getting There

From the center of Royalston, take Route 68 north 0.5 mile. Entrance and parking are on the left.

(One of the easiest ways to get to the center of Royalston is to exit Route 2 onto Route 202 north. Follow for 2.4 miles and turn left onto Route 68 north and travel 8.6 miles to the town's center.)

Open year-round, seven days a week, no admission fee, no rest rooms.

—M.T.

Doane's Falls

Royalston

31.5 acres

9/97

- 1 mile
- 30–40 minutes
- easy

The surging water at Doane's Falls is a thing of beauty but also one of danger. A visitor can't help but notice the large warning sign that lists the four teenagers who drowned here between 1960 and 1991. Cold water, dangerous currents, and no life guards mean these falls are for visual enjoyment, not swimming. Parents should also keep children away from the slippery ledges.

Now that the warnings are out of the way, enjoy a hike along one of the most impressive **waterfalls** in central Massachusetts. Begin your outing by taking the path that follows the water downstream adjacent to the falls. The falls are part of Lawrence Brook, which flows southwestward toward Tully Lake. In the spring, the brook gushes and swirls through the steep granite walls, and you walk with the roar of falling water in your ears.

There are plenty of spots to stop and take pictures of the falls; I like the shot looking back upstream of the water pouring from beneath the stone bridge. On the trail you will see an old **millstone** and stone blocks indicating this was once a mill site. According to The

Doane's Falls

N

1000 feet

Long Lake

Doane Hill Rd.

Athol Rd.

Lawrence Brook

mill site

P

mtn. Laurel

waterfalls

Chestnut Hill Ave.

Tully Lake

Trustees of Reservations (the nonprofit organization that owns this property), the first mill was built in 1753. At one time or another the falls powered a gristmill, a sawmill, a scouring and fulling mill, and a mill that produced wooden pails and tubs. The falls are named for the Doane family, who built the last mill here in the early 1800s. (On my walks through the state, I've found evidence of mills on almost every good-sized stream and river, even in places you would think had never been settled.)

At some places on the trail, you must pick your way through granite boulders of various sizes as you descend the gorge and the footing is a bit tricky. More waterfalls appear as you follow the trail downstream. (Looking at a topographical map, one can see how the brook is constricted by the steep terrain at the southern end of Jacobs Hill.)

The falls are shaded by pine and hemlock, and some of the trees are quite large, apparently saved from the logger's ax because of the difficulty of the terrain. The rest of the forest is comprised of white pine, maple, oak, and white birch.

Soon you will pass a branch of the trail on the right, and by continuing straight (close to the river), you arrive at a quiet pool where mountain laurel thickets surround the stream. In the late summer, look for the brilliant red petals of the cardinal flower. This slender, two- to four-foot plant grows along stream banks and other moist places.

The trail is rather faint here, but a 10-minute walk will lead you to where the stream enters Tully Lake. There is a nice southwest-facing slope here to sit on and soak up the sun. The waters of the lake are shallow, and you may see waterfowl bobbing on the surface. Early morning hikers may see **beavers** in this area. The beaver is one of the recent environmental success stories in

Massachusetts, after having been trapped out of existence in the 1800s. The Massachusetts Division of Fisheries and Wildlife started reintroducing beavers in the 1940s, and today they have spread to most areas of the state.

My most powerful memory of a beaver occurred during an evening fishing outing when I was in college. A group of us were bass fishing and having good luck as the last remnant of daylight sank behind the western horizon. Crickets were chirping, and the woods seemed

Spring snowmelt swells the brook near Doane's Falls.

a peaceful place until the water literally exploded in front of us. I'm sorry to say I dropped my fishing rod and ran for cover; it seemed like a boulder had landed in the water. At the time I had never heard the "thwack!" of a beaver's tail, a sound you don't forget in the dark. The beaver was telling us this was its pond, and we were intruders.

Tully Lake, which stretches out before you, covers approximately 300 acres and was built by the U.S. Army Corps of Engineers in 1947. The lake is surrounded by 1,250 acres of public land, supervised by the Commonwealth of Massachusetts Department of Environmental Management. Fishing for warm-water species is very productive on the lake, and there is a boat launch off Route 32 (10 horsepower limit).

By following the trail to the right (north) you will reach Doane Hill Road in 5 or 10 minutes. From there you can walk up the road to the east to reach your car, or retrace your steps back on the wooded trail along Lawrence Brook.

If you wish for more exploration, you can cross Doane Hill Road and follow the trail behind the yellow gate. This trail leads northward along the narrow part of Tully Lake for about a mile and half toward Long Lake and Spirit Falls. Another option is to return to your car and follow a trail that parallels Lawrence Brook in an upstream direction. More remains of mills can be seen, and the water moves quickly beneath hemlocks, pines, and maples.

Getting There

These directions first take you past Tully Lake and dam. From the intersection of Routes 2A and 32 in Athol, take Route 32 north 4.5 miles, and just beyond the dam at Tully Lake turn right on Doane Hill Road. Go to the end of the road and turn right. Parking is immediately on the right.

The Trustees of Reservations guidebooks offers an alternative way to reach the property: "From intersection of Route 2A and 32 in Athol, cross the Millers River bridge and bear right on Royalston-Athol Road. Proceed 4 miles. Entrance is on left after the stone bridge over Lawrence Brook, at intersection with Doane Hill Road."

Open year-round, seven days a week, no admission fee, no rest rooms.

—M.T.

Elliot Laurel Reservation

Phillipston

33 acres

10/18/97

- • 1 mile
- • 35 minutes
- • easy

Elliot Laurel Reservation lives up to its name; the **mountain laurel** that blankets the southern end of the property is truly impressive. If possible, time your trip to coincide with the blooming period in June. The reservation also has mature stands of hemlock, a red maple swamp, and a meadow.

Begin your walk on the main trail that passes through an opening in a stone wall adjacent to the parking area. Before entering the woods take a moment to scan the adjacent **field** for signs of wildlife. This is a good spot to observe deer, fox, rabbit, and maybe even a coyote. Not too long ago I had the thrill of seeing a **coyote** on the property. I was surprised at the size of the canine—larger than a fox—and I realized why they are sometimes called "little wolves." Coyote have expanded their range throughout Massachusetts and have even been sighted on Cape Cod. (In the winter, with the aid of a telescope, it sometimes is possible to spot a pack of coyote at nearby Quabbin Reservoir when they cross the ice or look for carrion. The Enfield Lookout is a good viewing spot.)

As soon as you enter the woods of Elliot Laurel you will notice the dark green leaves of the mountain laurel beneath the white pines and hemlocks. I love the enclosed feeling of walking through thick stands of lau-

The ofield near the entrance to Elliot Laurel is a good spot to watch for deer, fox, rabbit, and even coyote.

rel—it seems to add a bit of enchantment to the woods. Its flowers are saucer shaped, grow in dense clusters, and usually remain on the stems into mid-July. Colors range from white to pink to rose. Mountain laurel is sometimes confused with rhododendron, but the easiest way to tell them apart is by the leaves: laurel leaves are only 3 to 4 inches long, while rhododendron leaves are as long as 10 inches with a greater width.

The path forks a few feet down the trail; stay to the right, following an old stone wall that separates the woods from the field to your right. Soon there will be another fork and again you should stay right. Chipmunks and red squirrels are often seen in this evergreen forest. The feisty red squirrel is especially at home here, eating the buds of evergreens and the pine nuts. They usually den in old tree stumps, crevices, or underground dens, and sometimes make nests in trees using twigs and leaves. It's likely there are **flying squirrels** living in the area, but because they are nocturnal, they are difficult to see. I once was fortunate to view a flying squirrel up close and personal—it had hitched a ride inside by sleeping in our Christmas tree! Flying squirrels glide through the air by spreading skin flaps that stretch from the wrists to the ankles.

When the trail reaches the back of the field, it turns left (a faint trail from the field also enters on the right here) and soon begins to climb a bit, passing exposed ledges of granite covered with moss, ferns, and lichen. Yellow paint dots on a few trees help guide you along. This can be a beautiful area in the fall because the few maple trees scattered about really stand out against the dark evergreens. Winter also has its charm as the laurels' evergreen foliage sparkles against a backdrop of white snow.

About 20 minutes (three-quarters of a mile) into your walk, the trail begins to descend the hill you have been climbing and heads in a westerly direction. It was on this section of the property that I once got a glimpse of a goshawk, the largest member of the accipiter family. They are rapid-flying hawks at home winging through thick forest understory hunting for birds, squirrels, and other small mammals. Look for a gray belly and broad white eye stripe on this 19-inch-long accipiter. In my opinion they are the most magnificent of all the hawks.

Should you see one and it gives a high-pitched "auk, auk, auk," back away so as not to disturb its nest or territory. Goshawks will swoop down and attack intruders that threaten nesting areas.

After another 10 minutes of walking, the trail will bear south. On your right is a **red maple swamp.** Medium-sized trees, growing 50 to 75 feet tall, they are typically found in poorly drained places but can also grow in drier habitats. The bark of young red maples (also called swamp maples) is smooth and light gray, while older trees have dark gray bark that is ridged and broken into scales. Although there is no trail toward the swamp, I sometimes bushwack 50 yards along the ridge and rest against a rock on the hillside. Blue jays, chickadees, and titmice will usually keep you company, even in the winter. You never know what other forms of wildlife may happen past.

Back on the trail, walk through a stately stand of **hemlocks,** where little vegetation grows beneath the sweeping branches. Between an absence of sun and the acidity caused by the hemlock leaves, few plants can tolerate those conditions. The mountain laurel, however, does well in acidic, sandy soil in semishaded areas. Hemlock can be identified by its needles, which have blunt tips and are shorter than fir and most spruce. The branches are pendulous and will sway away from prevailing winds. Cones are light brown and about three-quarters of an inch long, hanging from the tips of tiny branchlets.

Bear left where a faint trail comes in on the right, and then in a short distance, the trail you are following intersects with the trail you started on. Simply bear right and you will be back at the car in five minutes. Elliot Laurel Reservation was given to The Trustees of Reservations in 1941 by Fredrick W. Elliot in memory of his mother. It is open to all for nature study, walking, and cross-country skiing.

Getting There

From Route 2 west, take Exit 21. Bear right at intersection, and follow Route 2A west 1.1 miles. Bear left at intersection, and follow Route 101 south 3.9 miles. Entrance is on the right.

From intersection of Routes 32 and 101 in Petersham, take Route 101 north 3.7 miles. Entrance is on left.

Open year-round, seven days a week, no admission fee, no rest rooms.

—M.T.

Bear's Den
New Salem
6.4 acres

- 3/8 mile
- 25 minutes
- easy
- great for children

Situated along a back road in the charming town of New Salem, the **waterfall** at Bear's Den should not be missed if you are in the area. Beneath towering hemlocks, the Middle Branch of the Swift River cascades over a 10-foot drop into small dark pools—a great location for photography buffs to capture the beauty of falling water. (Toward midday, the sun's rays hit squarely on the waterfall, making this my favorite time for picture taking.) Because the walk is a short one, a visit to this reservation is best combined with exploring other nearby natural areas such as Buffam Falls (see p. 186) or North Common Meadow (see p. 75). The name Bear's Den was given to the area by a settler who shot a black bear here. Black bear are now uncommon near Quabbin, but their numbers are healthy just to the west, on the other side of the Connecticut River.

From the roadside parking area, a rocky path follows the slope downhill toward the river. About 200 yards down the trail, on the right, you can see a rock foundation of an **early gristmill.** Just about every moving body of water in Massachusetts during the seventeenth and eighteenth centuries hosted either a gristmill or lumber mill. The textile mills of the 1800s tended to be on larger rivers, often built over the site of the earlier mills.

Another 100 yards down the path will bring you to the river, which has carved out a small gorge through granite cliffs. The best view of the falls can be seen by following the trail to the left a few feet up a knoll. The water tumbles down either side of a rock outcrop, forming two falls, each perhaps 12 feet in height. Cool, damp air seems to have permanently settled over the falls, adding to the special feeling of this enchanting place.

Each season imprints its own distinct mood on Bear's Den. In the springtime, when the river flexes its muscle with snowmelt, the water roars over the jagged rocks, foaming white in the pools below. During summer the low water makes this the perfect spot to sit and cool your feet after a walk. Autumn's colors are somewhat muted by the ravine and many hemlocks, but small colorful splashes of deciduous trees can be as beautiful in

A small waterfall is split by a boulder as it tumbles down.

their singularity as a whole forest ablaze. And winter's white blanket of snow and sparkling ice create a perfect contrast to the granite walls that rise darkly from the river's bottom.

You can climb the cliff above the falls, then follow a faint path alongside the river in an upstream direction. The stately **hemlocks** seem to grow right out of the granite, and **mountain laurel** is scattered in their understory. Fox, deer, wild turkey, raccoon, and fisher all live in these forested hills. **Fisher** do a good job of avoiding people—I've seen only one in all my hikes. They are deadly hunters, covering considerable ground, and in the winter it's possible to find their tracks and follow their trails as they search for mice, squirrels, rabbits, birds, and even porcupines to eat. Look for tracks that zigzag through the woods, stopping at rotten trees in search of rodent homes. Chances are, these are fisher tracks or those of another member of the weasel family.

The heavily forested land you are exploring is also good habitat for ruffed grouse, several species of owls, goshawks, and many smaller birds, such as thrushes, warblers, and many types of woodpeckers. **Ruffed grouse** prefer to winter in heavy conifers; they are a nonmigratory bird, 14 inches long, with rust and gray feathers with a black terminal band on the tail. When flushed they can burst into full flight (which can really startle you) but usually only travel a short distance before touching down again. The "drumbeat" you may hear in the woods is actually the male grouse beating its wings rapidly, trying to attract a female. As fascinating as this sound is, it is the female that is more interesting to me. More than once during a spring walk, I've come upon a female grouse that appeared to have an injured wing. The grouse was feigning injury to distract me from her tiny chicks, which blend in well with the brown forest floor.

The riverside trail is not long. When it peters out, retrace your steps back to the falls. It is said that during King Philip's War (1675–76), the Native Americans under the leadership of the Wampanoag sachem Philip (whose tribal name was Metacomet) gathered here. Nearby towns such as Deerfield, Northfield, and Hadley were all attacked and put to the torch by Wampanoag and Nipmuck warriors during the first few months of the war. Later, when the war turned in favor of the colonists, it is possible warriors may have congregated here. They were driven from their camp along the Connecticut River after a battle with the colonists.

Today, this small reservation is the picture of tranquillity and open for all to explore. It is through the generosity of a Mrs. Grais Poole Burrage that we have this land to enjoy. In *Saving Special Places: A Centennial History of the Trustees of Reservations,* author Gordon Abbott Jr. writes, "It was her (Mrs. Burrage) life long wish to have the Bear's Den remain as it had throughout the centuries, a magic and mystical place to be enjoyed by all."

Getting There

From Route 2 take Exit 16 to Route 202 south. Go 2.0 miles to the intersection of Routes 122 and 202 in New Salem, then take Route 202 south another 0.4 mile. Go right on Elm Street 0.7 mile, then left on Neilson Road 0.5 mile. Park on the roadside by the welcome sign on the right.

Open year-round, seven days a week, no admission fee, no rest rooms.

—M.T.

North Common Meadow
Petersham
24.5 acres

- **1.25 miles**
- **40 minutes**
- **easy**

North Common Meadow may be small in size but it has big rewards for those who walk its fields. The meadow is filled with **wildflowers** and a trail leads down to a quiet pond by the edge of woods. This combination of open fields, freshwater, and woods provides excellent habitat for birds such as meadowlarks, bobolinks, red-winged blackbirds, and passing hawks and owls. Adjacent to the property is the Brooks Woodland Preserve, where forested trails follow the clear-flowing waters of the East Branch of the Swift River.

Your walk begins at the trail next to the Brooks Law Office (built in 1835), which has a few beautiful old maples scattered around it. This spot offers a fine vista of the entire meadow and the pond below. I love the view in the spring, when many wildflowers are blooming, and again in autumn, when maples flame red and goldenrod blankets the slope near the pond.

The upper part of the meadow is a hay field that is mowed, and the lower section, closer to the pond, is a wildflower meadow. In the eighteenth and nineteenth

North Common Meadow

TO BROOKS WOODLAND

stream

Brooks Law Office

P

Route 32

apple trees

pond

field

East Street

Town Hall

N

200 feet

centuries, this is how most of Massachusetts looked; much of the state had been cleared for farming or pastureland, and very few trees escaped the ax. The forests that now cover most of the region are second and third growth, with only a few isolated acres still in virgin condition.

The meadow gently slopes down toward the pond, and a trail has been cut through the field. In just a few feet the trail forks; head to the left. Pass bluebird houses erected on poles. **Eastern bluebirds** prefer an open field like this, and it's important that the entrance hole is only one and a half inches across, enabling bluebirds to enter but keeping out larger birds, such as starlings. The male bluebird is the more colorful of the sexes with dark blue on the head, back, wings, and tail. Its throat is reddish brown and its belly is white. The female has light reddish coloring extending from chin over breast and back along flanks. Its head is light gray tinged with blue, and its back is dull brownish gray. Blue on the tail and wings is not always seen when the bird is perched.

Meadowlarks and **bobolinks** also prefer fields such as these. In the fall you might see a concentration of bobolinks near the marsh area as they gather for the fall migration. They resemble house sparrows but have crown stripes and narrow tail feathers. In the spring the male's underside is almost black, but as summer approaches it turns tan. The eastern meadowlark is identified by a black V on a bright yellow breast with white outer tail feathers. Meadowlarks are a joy to watch in flight, flapping and sailing above the meadow Thoreau makes mention of meadow larks and bluebirds in his essay *The Natural History of Massachusetts,* writing that "the plaintive note of the lark comes clear and sweet from the meadow: and the bluebird, like an azure ray, glances past us in our walk."

The trail passes some old apple trees, then leaves the hay field and enters the meadow of wildflowers. On my last visit, in mid-September, the asters and goldenrod made a kaleidoscope of purples and yellows, mixing with the browns and various shades of green from grasses and clover. Butterflies rose from the flowers by the side of the trail.

Where the path meets the woods at the stone wall, bear right toward the pond. If you were to go straight, you would be entering the Brooks Woodland Preserve (more about the preserve at the end of this chapter). Follow the trail to the edge of the small **pond** by a tiny stream and stop to scan the cattails and lily pads that

A cottontail rabbit nibbles on grass at North Common Meadow.

grow from its water. Some shadbush, dogwood, and iris grow near the pond's edge. Be on the lookout for frogs, turtles, wood ducks, and swallows.

The path forks near the southern end of the pond; the trail to the left makes a small loop and rejoins the trail. From the pond it is a 10-minute walk to East Street. Here you can either head back to your car by following East Street, or follow a path paralleling East Street that eventually leads to another path heading north through the hay field back toward your car. Wildflowers most easily identified will be the showy clusters of the tiny yellow-rayed flowers of goldenrod and blue or violet flowers of aster that grow singly rather than in tight clusters.

I prefer to walk on East Street, a quiet country lane, because it leads into the center of Petersham, one of the loveliest towns in the commonwealth. Most of the buildings that ring the town common are on the National Register of Historic Places, and many are in the Greek Revival style with white pillars. You can stop in at the Country Store for a cold beverage in the summer, or during the winter try a piece of pie with a hot drink.

(The Brooks Woodland Preserve is a wonderful place to explore and is comprised of two tracts. The Roaring Brook Tract can be accessed from the previously mentioned spot at North Common Meadow or by going down East Street 0.8 mile from Petersham center. To reach the Swift River Tract, follow Route 32 south from Petersham center to the intersection of Routes 32 and 122. Go south on Routes 32/122 for 1.5 miles, then turn left on Quaker Drive. There are two entrances on both sides of the bridge over the East Branch of the Swift.

This is a large property, more than 500 acres, and the wildlife is quite diverse. It is hilly country forested with hemlock, ash, maple, beech, birch, and white pine. There are scattered boulders and several outcroppings of rock. It will take you multiple trips to explore all the trails, but once you make your first visit, chances are you will be back soon.)

Getting There

From Route 2, take Exit 16 to Route 202 south. Go 2.0 miles to the intersection of Routes 202 and 122. Take Route 122 south about 8.0 miles to its intersection with Route 32. Turn onto Route 32 heading north and reach Petersham center in about a quarter of a mile. Just beyond the town green on Route 32 you will see the Brooks Law Office and North Common Meadow on your right. Pull off the road and park here.

Open year-round, seven days a week, no rest rooms.
—M.T.

Swift River Reservation

Petersham

439 acres

(The reservation is comprised of three separate tracts of land)

Slab City Tract—

10/18/97

- **1.75 miles**
- **1 hour, 15 minutes**
- **medium**
- **great for children**

The Slab City Tract at the Swift River Reservation (managed by The Trustees of Reservations) features a combination that's hard to beat: a clear-flowing river, old-growth timber, and a hilltop offering a far-reaching vista. The East Branch of the Swift River passes through the reservation and is a good spot to see wood ducks, heron, and beaver. If you arrive early you might see a deer, fox, or coyote cross the field near the parking area. Porcupine and ruffed grouse have also been seen here, although they tend to stay in the woods.

To begin your outing, follow the woods road from the parking area about 500 yards to where another old woods road enters on the left. Take this left, which leads up through a field and past an **old cellar hole** on the left. The cellar hole once supported the home of Avery Williams, who operated a sawmill on the river in the

Swift River Reservation
Slab City Tract

ledge

Connor Pond

cellar hole

animal enclosure

P

birch stand

logging road

79   78

Route 122/32

giant pines and hemlocks

Swift River

N

gate

80

500 feet

mid-1800s. Nearby is a rectangular stone enclosure where the farm animals were kept. Soon after these signs of the old Avery mill and farm, the road forks. Bear left, toward the river, which has spilled into a broad marsh. There are a couple of spots where you can view the marsh, perhaps observing the head of a swimming muskrat or beaver. The trail parallels the marsh to where the river exits the wetlands, passing beneath **enormous hemlocks and white pines,** only about 15 minutes from the start of the walk.

I've always thought this was one of the most beautiful **river walks** in all the Bay State. The Swift courses over rocks and around boulders, seeming to sing on its way to fill the Quabbin. Take a moment to sit by the river and feel the peace of this enchanting spot. Look for the ring of rising trout as they feed on insects that have either fallen in the water or hatched from the streambed.

The hemlocks and pines here are home to red squirrel, raccoon, fisher, and owl. Though their population was reduced by the rabies epidemic of the 1990s, you will still find **raccoons.** They are most active at sundown when they prowl about in search of food. Their food is quite varied—toads, frogs, crayfish, grubs, turtle and birds' eggs, and plants (anyone growing corn knows the 'coon's perfect timing for raiding a garden). In the wintertime, raccoons may sleep for many days in protected places, such as hollow trees, to withstand the coldest temperatures. While they do not actually hibernate and sometimes venture out of their nests, raccoons may lose up to 50 percent of their fall body weight during the course of the winter.

The river trail extends for about a quarter of a mile and then ends at a green gate, marking the reservation's boundary. About 20 feet before the gate is a narrow trail on the right that zigzags uphill, away from the river. (There will be a marker #80 nailed to a tree.) Take this trail, and follow the yellow paint dots on the trees marking its path. This seems to be an area favored by **grouse,** and more than once I've been surprised by one suddenly exploding skyward. There are only a few evergreens mixed with small maples, and in the fall you can see through the understory. You might catch a glimpse of a deer's white tail as it bounds off.

Continue on this narrow path until it intersects with a logging road at marker #78 where a power line crosses the trail (about a 15-minute walk from the river). To reach the **scenic overlook,** turn left here and then bear right where the road forks at marker #79. To the south and east, the woods are owned by The Trustees of Reservations, while ahead, to the north, the property is part of the Harvard Forest. It's only a 10-minute gradual climb (passing a private field on the left and a nice stand of birch on the right) until you should turn right on a small path that leads to the outcrop of rock at the overlook. (This can be a difficult trail to spot—look for it just before a large section of exposed rock ledge on the right.)

This is one of my favorite hilltops. Few people seem to know about the place and you usually have the summit all to yourself. Roughly half the summit is open ledge, allowing for an unobstructed view to the east. The body of water seen below is Connor Pond. Beyond that, the wooded hills are part of Massachusetts Audubon's Rutland Brook Sanctuary, a property designated for wildlife only. Along the ridge where you are standing, I've seen lots of porcupine signs. In the winter you may see tracks and nipped hemlock boughs. Porcupines den in the nooks and crannies of the rock ledge, and in this general area it's possible to see porcupine scat near the entrance to these little caves.

After enjoying the view, retrace your steps to marker #78 near the power line. Instead of turning right on

A young hiker rests on a granite ledge at Swift River Reservation.

the trail you came up, you can go straight down this woods road for a shortcut to the parking area. Maples and hemlocks line the power line path. (During one of my hikes I had the rare treat of seeing a goshawk perched in a tree where the woods meet the field at the end of this road.) It's only a 15- to 20-minute downhill walk to your car, covering about half a mile.

More ambitious walkers may want to explore another tract of the Swift River Reservation. The Davis Tract is located off Glen Valley Road, and it, too, has a scenic overlook and river trail. Cellar holes and stone walls remind walkers of the days when these woods were cleared for pasture. The Nichewaug Tract is on the north side of Swift River, and its entrance is found on Nichewaug Road. Miles of trails lead through woods and old pastures. Like the others, Nichewaug Tract has a ledge outcrop offering a scenic view. Together, the three sections total 439 acres of wild lands—secluded enough for larger animals such as black bear, bobcat, and coyote. And if you are really lucky, you just might spot a moose. An increasing number of sightings have occurred in this area, and tracks have been seen at the Swift River Reservation. Bring your camera!

Getting There

All areas are between Nichewaug Road and Routes 122/32.

Slab City Tract: from intersection of Routes 122 and 32, south of Petersham center, go south on Routes 122/32, 2.0 miles to Connor Pond. Entrance is on the right, across from the dam.

Nichewaug Tract: from intersection of Routes 122 and 32, south of Petersham center, take South Street 0.9 mile. Turn right on Nichewaug Road and travel 0.6 mile. Entrance is on left.

Davis Tract: from intersection of Routes 122 and 32, south of Petersham center, go south on Routes 122/32, 3.3 miles. Turn right on Glen Valley Road and proceed 0.9 mile to intersection of Carter Pond Road. Entrance is on the right.

Open year-round, seven days a week, no admission fee, no rest rooms.

—M.T.

Quabbin Reservoir Gate 45

Hardwick
(119 miles of shoreline surround
entire reservoir)

3/23/97

- 2.5–3 hours
- 5 miles
- moderate

For the outdoors lover, the forests of Quabbin Reservoir
are nothing short of paradise. The 39-square-mile reservoir, one of the largest reservoirs in the world built for
domestic supply, has 119 miles of shoreline, not including the many islands rising from its depths. Quabbin
means "meeting of the waters" in the Nipmuck lan-
guage, and before the creation of the reservoir this valley
was exactly that. The three branches of the Swift River
converged here, making the valley the ideal spot for a
reservoir. The fact that people lived in the valley did not
stop the city of Boston from getting the water it needed.
The towns of Enfield, Prescott, Dana, and Greenwich
were "drowned" when dams were constructed at the
valley's southern end.

There is a silver lining to the flooding of the Swift
River valley—the watershed needs protection and thousands of surrounding acres have been left in their natural state, open only for passive recreation such as walk-

Quabbin Reservoir
Gate 45

ing. The wildlife here is diverse and abundant, and for that reason I've been a regular visitor to the reservoir during the past 20 years. With so many entry gates to choose from, each trip finds me at a different gate, discovering a new trail, new stream, or new meadow. Gate

45 is a fascinating area. It's one of the less frequented entrances into the forest, and the walk described here leads to the **reservoir** itself, with a return stop at a **beaver pond** where great blue herons nest.

After parking your car on the shoulder of Lyman Road at Gate 45, go around the gate and start your walk down this old roadway. The **fieldstone** walls that line the road might cause you to reflect on how this land looked prior to the reservoir's creation. Farms and small mills dotted the valley. The acres around you were probably pastures before the start of construction of the reservoir in 1928. Some of the original **maples** that shaded the road are still standing along the stone wall, while the woods beyond are filled with younger pines and oaks.

Five minutes into the walk you will pass an open area on the left— a good spot to look for deer. (White-tailed deer were so numerous in the watershed that a limited—and controversial—form of hunting was recently allowed.) The field is also a good place to spot **fox** hunting for mice and various hawks doing the same. Red foxes are bright yellowish red on the sides to deep yellowish brown on the back, with a long bushy tail tipped white. The best time to see them is at dawn or dusk, although sometimes, especially in the spring when mothers must hunt for food for their young, they are seen in the middle of the day. Besides fox, I often see ruffed grouse here (sometimes they will remain still as you unknowingly walk closer; then they suddenly spring up, scaring the wits out of you—it's happened more than once to me!).

After walking about 20 minutes, pass a road on your right, about three-quarters of a mile from the start of your walk. Keep its location in mind for the return walk from the reservoir. Proceed straight ahead through a wooded area with many white pines, and pass a **beaver pond** on the left. With the aid of binoculars, you might glimpse a beaver, but these fascinating animals are mostly nocturnal. Legend has it that beavers are smart enough to fell a tree in the direction they want it to go. In reality, the trees fall haphazardly, sometimes even crushing the beaver. An adult will cut down about one tree every two days (staying within 200 to 300 feet of the safety of water) and feed on the bark. In the autumn they stockpile green branches near the lodge to serve as a food cache through the winter.

Continue to follow the road in a westerly direction, first passing by a small plantation of red pine on the left. (Lots of red squirrels can be seen near these evergreens.) Soon the road arcs left and a **stream** rushes beneath the road through old stone culverts. Reach an intersection with another road and follow it to the right, downhill through a dense, **dark hemlock grove.** Hemlock has a more rounded top than spruces or firs, and its twigs and branches are more flexible. (You may want to first follow the brook upstream into the forest—this stream flows out of the beaver pond you passed, and you never know what wildlife you might encounter prowling the banks of the waterway.)

Walk downhill on the old road. The stream keeps you company, singing over small falls as it makes its way to fill the Quabbin. I've seen porcupines feeding in the hemlocks near here. It is a good idea to glance upward into the trees occasionally for signs of these large prickly rodents. Porcupines consume a large amount of hemlock foliage, and oftentimes a particular hemlock will be completely stunted by browsing porcupine. Soon you will pass a few handsome white birch on the right and then you will arrive at the shores of Quabbin, roughly 50 minutes (two miles) after leaving your car. Follow the trail to the left, adjacent to the shore, and in a few hundred feet the stream appears again, cascading down the hillside and spilling into the Quabbin at a beautiful half-moon beach.

This is a wonderful spot to pause and rest your eyes on the blue waters of the reservoir. Directly across from you is an **island**—once a hilltop—called Mt. Lizzie, just one of 60 islands in the reservoir. Stretching in a north-south direction, Quabbin is almost 18 miles long and has a capacity of 412 billion gallons of water. (Just an inch of rainfall can add 750 million gallons to the reservoir.) The water is quite deep in spots, and the depth at the Winsor Dam is 150 feet, making this one of the premier cold-water fisheries in New England. (Fishing is permitted on much of the reservoir, but swimming is not allowed.)

Winter at Quabbin is an especially interesting time. Bald eagles and coyotes are sometimes seen out on the ice feeding on the carcasses of deer. Not only do **eagles** winter at Quabbin, but there are also nesting eagles here in the warm-weather months, a result of many years of effort to restore this magnificent bird to our state. Biologists brought six- to seven-week-old chicks to Quabbin and raised them on an elevated platform. When they were able to fly, they were released (with Quabbin imprinted as their home), and they later returned to build their own nests.

Although you might spot an eagle with the aid of binoculars from the shore, the best bet for observation is at the Enfield Lookout, near the dams. Usually someone is patiently waiting and watching with high-powered binoculars or a spotting scope, and most birders are happy to let you have a look. When the reservoir is not socked in by ice, the eagles soar over the water in search of fish, their primary source of food. With a wingspread of seven to eight feet and the unmistakable white head and tail on mature birds, a soaring bald eagle is one of the most impressive sights in the wild.

The fascinating **common loon** also visits and nests at Quabbin. Like the eagle, loons seek out the reservoir

Quabbin is one of the few places in Massachusetts frequented by moose.

because of its vast expanse of open waters and the many secluded sections off-limits to the public. Both birds feed on fish—the eagle skims the surface to snatch a fish and the loon dives underwater and catches fish with its sharp beak. Cruising slowly on the surface, loons will stick their heads underwater looking for fish, then dive like dolphins, often chasing a fish for more than 45 seconds. Loons once nested throughout Massachusetts, but human encroachment led to loss of habitat and the birds were extirpated in the state by the early 1900s. Now there are a handful of nesting loons at Quabbin, and if the acid rain problem does not worsen, the outlook is considered good for increased numbers because large sections of Quabbin and other reservoirs are closed to boating. More than once I've heard their unmistakable, haunting cry rise over the waters of Quabbin.

You might want to walk the shoreline a bit, examining the smooth, twisted forms of driftwood and the many waterworn tree stumps that look like giant spiders. The patches of sand at the water's edge usually show the print of deer hooves and sometimes the tracks of other animals such as coyote, otter, raccoon, mink, and fisher. On two of my trips to the reservoir I've seen raccoons foraging among the rocks, presumably for mussels or crayfish.

When you retrace your steps to the car be sure to explore the side road mentioned earlier (as you return it will be on your left, just 20 minutes from Gate 45). This road leads to a large beaver pond after only a 15- to 20-minute walk. While the beaver engineers its surroundings for its own protection, a by-product of its work is a pond that becomes home to other wildlife such as otter and wood ducks. Perhaps the biggest beneficiary is the great blue heron, who uses the standing timber in the pond for safe and secure nest platforms. On my last visit, this pond had two heron nests. Nests are up to four feet wide and are made of sticks and branches. Although the nests look precarious, they hold up well year after year. In the springtime a heron rookery is an active place, with both parents feeding the young a diet of regurgitated fish and frogs twice a day.

Getting There

From the Massachusetts Turnpike take the Palmer-Route 32 exit. Proceed north on Route 32 through Ware, and then continue north on Route 32A into Hardwick. Across from the Hardwick town common on the left is Greenwich Road. Follow Greenwich Road 2.6 miles until you reach Gate 43. Bear left at Gate 43 (staying on Greenwich Road) and go 1.7 miles to Lyman Road on the right. Follow Lyman Road 0.7 mile to Gate 45 and park off the road. (Lyman Road can be slippery in periods of snow and ice. If conditions are bad, try Gate 43, Gate 40, or Quabbin Hill near the Winsor Dam.)

Open year-round, seven days a week, no fee, no rest rooms.

—M.T.

Rock House Reservation
West Brookfield
75 acres

1/97
many times since

- **1.5 miles**
- **45 minutes**
- **easy**
- **great for children**

Rock House Reservation is a "must see." On the property is a 20- to 30-foot **rock shelter,** known as the Rock House, that was used by Native Americans as a hunting camp in the cold-weather months. One look at this sloping ledge of rock and it's easy to see the advantages it offers—protection from wind and snow and a southeast-facing opening to catch the warmth of the sun. (The rock ledge could also have been used as a defensive fortification.) Because of the property's historical significance and the imprint left by retreating glaciers, the Rock House Reservation, managed by The Trustees of Reservations, is a good place to introduce children to New England heritage and geology. And the nooks and crannies within the rock shelter will delight little explorers!

The property's diverse habitats offer great opportunity for nature study. It has a pond, a pine and spruce stand, and upland woods of hemlock, maple, and oak, where glacial boulders are scattered over the hilly land-

Rock House Reservation

Summit Trail

power lines

N

350 feet

balance rock

Trailside Museum

Inner Loop Trail

Outer Loop Trail

red pine and spruce

Inner Loop Trail

pond

Fire Road

Rock House

dam

stream

Inner Loop Trail

P

Route 9

Rock House

scape. It is an especially interesting spot to visit in the winter because few people seem to hike beyond the Rock House, making **wildlife tracking** relatively easy along the reservation's many trails.

Begin your walk by following Inner Loop Trail uphill directly behind the signboard at the edge of the parking area. Within five minutes you will see the pond. Bear left along the edge of the pond, where the trail splits, and the Rock House will be on your left. Take a few moments to explore the shelter, and if it's winter, note how the ground immediately below the overhanging rock is free of snow. The shelter, probably formed by the glaciers, looks like a giant lean-to. It is surmised that Native Americans camped here over a 7,000-year period. An amateur archaeological dig in the 1930s revealed early tools, pottery, and bones from wolf, bear, and deer.

Let your imagination picture the various uses of the Rock House by these early hunters. Perhaps they lit fires beneath the overhang, letting the rock walls reflect the warmth of the flames. Maybe logs and boughs were erected in the front of the shelter to keep out eastern winds or to serve as protection against wolves and enemy tribes. On one winter visit, I sat on the dry ground beneath the overhang and reflected on all the other souls that had rested in the same spot, wondering what kind of thoughts and dreams they had.

The **glacier** that covered New England formed as snow fell almost continuously to our north in Quebec. The snowpack grew over a mile high, and weight of the pile squeezed the snow at the bottom into ice. Then the massive pile of ice and snow began to slide south, smoothing northern sides of mountains as it advanced and leaving rougher surfaces and rubble when it retreated about 15,000 years ago. Note the smooth northern side of the granite hill of the Rock House and the rougher cliff face forming the shelter on the southern end.

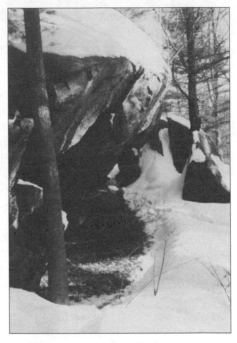

The large rock overhang keeps the snow from reaching the sheltered area below.

After exploring the nooks and crannies of the Rock House, continue your walk by following the path along the **pond** in a northerly direction. The trail intersects with a fire road where you should bear right, following the road as it climbs above the pond. On your right you will soon see a small yellow cottage. Inside is a trailside museum (open year-round) where you can learn more about the property. From the porch of the cottage, look down upon the pond. This is a good spot to have a snack or, if it's autumn, admire the colors of the maples and oak that ring the pond. From this vantage point you might see beaver, wild turkey, screech owls, and fox.

When you walk back to the fire road, continue northeast passing the Inner Loop Trail, but keep an eye out to the right for Balance Rock. A five-foot boulder rests at the top of a rock ledge—yet another unique geological formation caused by glacial movement. (As the glaciers retreated, boulders were deposited haphazardly, like this one, and are called erratics.) Kids will love climbing to the top of the ledge to see this oddity. While my kids tried to push Balance Rock (no chance of moving the giant boulder), I admired the huge oak that grows directly below this craggy outcrop.

Back on the fire road it's only a five-minute walk farther to the northeast until you will see a power line ahead. Follow the trail to the right, called the Outer Loop Trail, just before the power line. If you were to continue on the fire road and then take a left onto the Summit Trail, you would reach a ridge with a vista within a 25-minute walk.

The Outer Loop Trail circles to the southeast, first passing through a plantation of **red pine, Norway spruce,** and **red spruce.** Red pine has four- to six-inch flexible dark green needles, and the bark has flat ridges and shallow grooves on it. Norway spruce has much smaller needles of a half inch to one inch and has drooping branches. The needles of a red spruce are smaller still, one-half inch to five-eighths of an inch long, and are often curved upward. The trail then passes through a wood of oak, white pine, maple, and a scattering of hemlock. Old stone walls lace the woodlands, indicating the farming activity here many years ago. Today the walls are home to chipmunks. I've also seen cottontails and porcupine tracks along the stone wall.

On one of my visits to Rock House I had the good fortune to meet Paul Gryzbowski and Dick O'Brien, who manage the Central Region properties for The Trustees of Reservations. They told me white-tailed deer, raccoon, coyote, and red fox have also been sighted on the property. One animal that few of us ever see but is likely to have hunted here is the **bobcat,** a secretive animal that ranges throughout the hills of the greater Quabbin area.

The bobcat is a solitary meat eater, active mostly at night. Its keen hearing and eyesight allows it to lie quietly in ambush until prey comes along. Cottontail and snowshoe rabbits are its chief source of food, although it sometimes eats mice, squirrels, grouse, muskrat, and birds. Occasionally a bobcat will take a young deer, either by stalking, lying in ambush, or even positioning itself in a tree above a deer run.

Bobcats den in rock crevices, hollow trees, or under fallen logs. They usually mate in February, and during this time they are known to make an eerie yowling sound. Their young are born in the early spring and are weaned when they are two months old, remaining with their mother through the summer before they go off on their own. If you should ever see one, consider it a special wildlife encounter.

Back on the Outer Loop Trail, it's only a half-mile walk from the start of this trail to its intersection with the Inner Loop Trail (turn left), and then another three or four minutes to the earthen dam at the base of the pond. Eastern water snakes and painted turtles sun themselves here. Be on the lookout for belted kingfisher and great blue heron hunting for small fish. A tiny stream leaves the pond here.

David Lahti studied the natural history of the property for The Trustees of Reservations and reported a beaver in the pond. He also spotted a mink running along the dam where you now stand. Many birds live on or pass through the 75 acres of Rock House Reservation, including red-tailed hawks, screech owls, scarlet tanager, downy and hairy woodpeckers, hermit thrush, and warblers.

From the pond, turn left at the end of the dam and retrace your original steps back to the parking area. If you visit in winter when the snow is deep, I recommend snowshoes rather than cross-country skis for the hilly, winding trails.

Getting There

From the Massachusetts Turnpike, take Exit 8 for Palmer. Go north on Route 32, into and through the center of Ware, where Routes 32 and 9 combine. When they separate, bear to the right and stay on Route 9 east for 1.2 miles to parking and entrance on the left.

Open year-round, seven days a week, no admission fee, no rest rooms.

—M.T.

Tantiusques Reservation
Sturbridge
55 acres

- **1.75 miles**
- **50 minutes**
- **easy**
- **great for children**

When one thinks of mining, the western United States usually comes to mind, but here at Tantiusques Reservation evidence of early **mining operations,** complete with a small mine shaft, is scattered throughout the wooded property. Since 1962 The Trustees of Reservations have owned and managed the property. Trails wind through the hills where white-tailed deer, raccoon, fox, ruffed grouse, and other animals make their home. You can either make a three-quarter-mile walk or extend your walk into the adjoining Massachusetts Wildlife Management Area.

The first excavation site for mining graphite is very close to the parking area. As you face the lone trail leading into the woods, an open cut into the rock is just beyond sight to your right, about 40 feet up a small hill, which can be easily climbed. Long before the white man arrived in the area, the local Nipmuck tribe chipped off the black ore to paint their faces for ceremonies. Later, when the settlers discovered the "black lead," they used metal picks and shovels to excavate the graphite sandwiched in the granite hills. (Graphite is softer than gran-

Tantiusques Reservation

MASSACHUSETTS WILDLIFE
MANAGEMENT AREA

Leadmine Rd.

open
mining
cut

tunnel

P

ridge

TRUSTEES
PROPERTY

open
mining

N

100 feet

ite and could be excavated with simple tools.)

A trapper and scout named John Oldham first arrived at the site in 1633. Ten years later the property was acquired by John Winthrop Jr., son of the first governor of Massachusetts Bay Colony. But Winthrop's dreams of a lucrative operation never came to pass. In

1658 some black lead was extracted from the site, as told in this letter from the elder Winthrop to his son: "There is some black lead digged, but not so much as they expected it being very difficult to gett out of ye rocks...."

After the property was sold by the Winthrop family in 1784, mining continued. Graphite was packed into barrels and taken to Boston on horse-drawn wagons. There it was loaded onto packet ships and sent to England. Operation of the mine ended in 1855.

By following the main trail from the parking area it is possible to see a tunnel into the rock hillside just five minutes down the path. Its opening is about four feet by four feet, and it is particularly interesting to see in winter when strange **formations of ice** rise from the floor. Apparently the roof of the cave leaks water, and the falling drops freeze into something that resembles stalagmites. (It is dangerous to enter the small shaft.)

The trail angles off in a southwestern direction through oaks, maples, and an understory of **mountain laurel.** Autumn colors here are quite beautiful: the maples provide shades of crimson and gold, while the browns of the oaks contrast with the glittering green leaves of the mountain laurel. Another trail forks off to the right, leading over a ridge, but continue straight ahead.

Soon another mining area appears. This excavation is not a cave but instead is a cut into the rock hillside. You can walk into this one. It, too, has beautiful ice formations in the winter, with huge icicles hanging from the rock ledges. When you walk through the cut, it's like being in a miniature canyon with rock walls about 25 feet high.

Back on the trail, the path narrows a bit and hemlock trees are now mixed with deciduous trees. About 15 minutes from the start of your walk, the trail turns toward the north. The trail is fairly level and, with adequate snow cover, would make for good cross-country skiing. On my winter trip there were no human tracks in the snow, but it was easy to see the prints of deer and **fox**. The red-tailed fox is one of nature's most handsome creatures. Consider yourself lucky should you see one, for they are quite secretive. Thoreau admired the fox, writing, "His recent tracks still give variety to a winter's walk. I tread in the steps of the fox that has gone before me by some hours, or which perhaps I have started, with such a tip-toe of expectation as if I were on the trail of the Spirit itself. . . . "

Fox are active hunters in the winter, following regular routes while searching for rabbit, partridge, and mice. They hunt alone, usually at night, and rarely range more than five miles from their home base. They use

Red-tailed fox kits play near their den.

dens primarily for the protection of their pups, which are born in late March and April in litters of 1 to 10 pups. I recently came across a den that had 7 pups playing on the mound of sand in front of the den.

The trail now leads northeast, passing the connecting trail that climbs the ridge to the right. Continue on the main trail and, soon after passing the connecting trail, enter a Massachusetts Wildlife Management Area (be aware that **hunting** is allowed there, and if you are visiting in the fall wear blaze orange). I always love to walk on a straight, level trail like this because for a few minutes I can forget where I am and just let the rhythm of walking take over. The feeling of not having a care in the world and putting your body on automatic pilot is just one of the many reasons why I take a walk in the woods every weekend.

After walking toward the northeast for 20 minutes, you will reach Leadmine Road, though you may have to pick your way around a few trees that have blown down. Simply turn right and follow the road for about 10 minutes to reach your car. The total walk seldom takes me longer than 50 minutes.

Getting There

From I-84 west take Exit 1, Mashapaug Road—Southbridge. Turn right off the exit ramp and follow Route 15 south for 1.5 miles. Turn right onto Leadmine Road and travel 0.9 mile to entrance on left.

Open year-round, seven days a week, no admission fee, no rest rooms.

—M.T.

Franklin County

Mt. Grace State Forest
Warwick
1,689 acres

4/5/97

snow shoeing
winter 98
- Bushwacked to top

- **2.8 miles**
- **3 hours**
- **difficult**

For exquisite fall foliage viewing, it is hard to surpass the **360-degree vista** from the tower atop 1,617-foot-high Mt. Grace in Franklin County, near the New Hampshire line. Thickly clothed in northern hardwoods, hemlock, and white pine, a sea of multihued woodland stretches for miles below you in all directions—northeast to Mt. Monadnock, south to Quabbin Reservoir, southwest to Mt. Tom, and west to Mt. Greylock. To obtain the views, however, you must climb the steel tower, which has been well maintained and is in good condition.

The elevation gain is a very respectable 1,047 feet—more than any other walk in this guide—but the Metacomet-Monadnock Trail (M-M Trail) is in fine shape, and you'll no doubt agree that the view is well worth the moderate exertion required. Allow about one and a half hours to reach the summit. Since this property is not much visited you may even have it all to yourself!

Mt. Grace State Forest

N

1/4 mile

Mountain Brook

P

Route 78

pond

MT. GRACE STATE FOREST

Bennetts Knob

Mt. Grace ▲

Northfield Rd.

power line

After leaving your locked vehicle at a dirt pull-off on the west side of Route 78, walk south for about 0.1 mile to the M-M Trail crossing. Turn right onto the trail and follow it west across Mountain Brook. Continue straight up into the woods on the old woods road. Walking gradually uphill you'll soon cross another brook; on your left will be a tiny rock-lined pond built by the Civilian Conservation Corps (CCC) in the 1930s. The brook flows away to the right and the trail levels out, leading you to an Adirondack shelter. Eastern phoebes have nested inside the structure—look for the remnants of this flycatcher's moss-covered mud nest.

The M-M Trail now swings left and uphill—look for the trademark white paint blazes. Walk through lovely woods of eastern hemlock, American beech, and red maple. Some of the hemlocks are quite large and there are many tiny trees pushing up from the forest floor; unlike many species, hemlocks are shade tolerant. There is not much ground cover here. The twin coral red berries and fingernail-sized leaves of creeping partridgeberry are numerous near the trail, however. Recross the small brook and continue to climb gradually over the wide track. Impish red-breasted nuthatches, sometimes tooting their tiny tin horns, reside and breed in the deep woodlands.

Cross another small brook and pass through a cool hemlock grove—the stream has cut a small gorge below and left. Continuing to climb steadily, the trail leads you through some rather large white pines. Energetic red squirrels gather the cones containing the delicious and nutritious winged seeds—some to be eaten now but most for future consumption. Mushrooms are also a favorite on the menu of this attractive tree squirrel. Red squirrels also eagerly seek out and eat birds' eggs, nestlings, and other high-protein animal foods. Farther up the trail you'll see a huge gray birch down to the right of the trail. At almost three feet in diameter, it may have been left to provide shade for livestock long ago. Gray birch superficially resembles white birch and many confuse the two species; **gray birch** does not peel as thinly or readily as white, and its whitish bark becomes increasingly gray and rough as it ages.

Terrestrial, sticky-skinned red-backed salamanders seek daytime refuge below the rotting logs of deciduous trees. By turning a few logs, you're sure to find some; be sure to carefully replace the log and salamander as you found them. In early October, the trail will be littered with the bright red leaves of red maple—a tree that can grow in wet, waterlogged soils as well as in dry ones.

Farther on, continue straight as a smaller, unmarked path enters from the right. The trail now becomes somewhat steeper and eventually swings to the left near the summit. Along this "terminal" portion grow lots of **trailing arbutus,** the Massachusetts state flower. Mayflower, as it is also known, quite appropriately blooms in May. Both late low blueberry (about one foot tall) and early low blueberry (up to three feet tall, with larger leaves) are common along the trail. Dirt Fire Tower Road meets the hiking trail on the left just below the summit. From the base of the tall tower the view is limited.

What a dramatic difference awaits as you ascend the eight tower levels for a completely unobstructed view in all directions. It's breathtaking. The fact that this area is

The sweeping panoramic view from the tower includes Mt. Monadnock in New Hampshire.

quite thinly populated is readily apparent. Photogenic in any season, it peaks during the height of the fall foliage season in early October. If you're lucky and the winds are out of the northwest, you may also see large numbers of migrant broad-winged and smaller, long-tailed sharp-shinned hawks drifting southward.

This is an excellent place to have lunch before heading back down the mountain. Little bluestem, a grass of the mid-continent tall grass prairies, and bushy hairgrass grow in the sunlight of the small clearing on the top of Mt. Grace. Blooming goldenrod attracts pollinating wasps, bees, and other insects to its yellow inflorescences in late summer and early fall. A bronze plaque commemorating the establishment of the State Forest in 1920 was affixed to a granite glacial erratic on the summit by the Civilian Conservation

Corps in the 1930s. The CCC completed a great deal of work in the forest as it did on many of the state's other conservation lands. The boulder also holds the names of CCC employees who left their chiseled marks there more than 55 years ago.

You have several options for the return trip. In addition to taking the most direct way—back the same way you came—you can follow a trail that leads east to a picnic area along Route 78 and then take a path from the picnic area back to your vehicle. The other choice is to follow a less easily found path that roughly parallels the M-M Trail on the opposite side of the ravine, back to the Adirondack shelter near the start of the route. In any case, retrace your steps back down the M-M Trail to start down.

If you do not wish to follow the M-M Trail down, take the narrow, unblazed trail that forks off of the M-M Trail less than two-tenths of a mile below the tower. Pass a lichen-covered glacial erratic on the left and come to another trail junction. The left one (orange paint blazes on trunks) leads down in a northeasterly direction, but the trail is not well maintained and it's easy to stray from the path. This path is not traveled much and the blazes, most low to the ground, are sporadic. Eventually it leads one back to the Adirondack shelter and the M-M Trail.

Staying to the right at the trail junction will take you to the vandalism-plagued picnic area (no tables) that borders Route 78 along Mountain Brook (which flows through a nicely constructed CCC rock-lined channel). From here, it's approximately half a mile north on a path that roughly parallels the west side of the highway to the parking area.

Allow about one hour for the descent on any trail.

Getting There

From the junction of Routes 2 and 2A in Erving, take Route 2A east for 2.1 miles to the junction with Route 78 on the left. Take Route 78 north for 7.4 miles to the State Forest headquarters—currently unstaffed—on the left just past the intersection of Route 78 and Athol Road. Continue north on Route 78 for 1.4 miles to a dirt pull-off on the left side of the road (approximately 0.3 mile before the junction with Robbins Road on the right).

Hours are dawn till dusk. No admission fee. No rest rooms currently available. Motorized vehicles (except snowmobiles) prohibited.

—R.L.

Northfield Mountain Recreation and Environmental Center
Northfield
2,200 acres

- 4.5 miles
- 4 hours
- moderate

Northfield Mountain is unique among properties covered by this guide. Three-hundred-acre Northfield Mountain Reservoir—atop the plateau between the Connecticut and Millers Rivers—is part of a Northeast Utilities pumped-storage facility that produces hydroelectric power during times of peak demand. Water is pumped 2.8 miles through a tunnel from the Connecticut River and up 800 vertical feet to the reservoir. When water is released, it drives the huge turbines of the subterranean power plant one-half mile below the surface. This process, which is capable of generating 1 million kilowatts of electricity, is explained by exhibits housed in the visitor center. Twenty-five miles of very well maintained and truly multiuse trails also set this operation apart.

Although significant portions of the property are in a highly altered state, there are ample opportunities here to explore extensive woodlands and to amble along scenic rock ledges with panoramic views. The property borders thousands of acres of forested lands, and thus virtually all the indigenous interior southern New England fauna is resident—from 0.15-ounce masked shrews to 400-pound black bears. The unvegetated banks of Northfield Mountain Reservoir are not a particularly attractive sight, but lovely Rose Ledge and Lower Rose Ledge Trails will make getting there the best part of the journey.

From the trailhead (elevation 283 feet) on the east side of the visitor center, where there is a large map of the trail system, walk toward the right around a small cattail-fringed pond, left. Light green filamentous algae—*Spirogyra*—provides cover and sustenance to minute pond invertebrates, which in turn feed more complex creatures such as frogs and red-spotted newts. Continue across the mowed area and enter a white pine stand straight ahead. Watch for blue plastic blazes on the trunks. There is very little plant growth—starflower and Canada mayflower being exceptions. Cross the cart road, swing left, and proceed under humming power lines, past a restricted area on the left to the beginning of Rose Ledge Trail (orange blazes), right. Hay-scented and New York ferns are common along the trail.

Horizontally bedded **gneiss rock outcrops** begin to appear. Cross Hemlock Hill cart road. Enter shady hemlock woods and cross a bridge over a brook. Next cross Jug End cart road and continue through hemlocks. The character of the forest changes to drier oak/maple/pine with an understory of mountain laurel and American chestnut. After crossing a bridge over an intermittent stream, pass Lower Rose Ledge Trail intersection on the right. Continue straight and proceed through woodlands composed largely of maple, birch, pignut hickory, and white pine. Tiny clubmosses (princess pine) and ferns dot the forest floor. Black-capped chickadees are among the most abundant birds year-round. From fall to spring they travel in family groups with other year-

Horizontally bedded ledges of granitic gneiss are dominant features along the trail.

round woodland residents—nuthatches, downy woodpeckers, and brown creepers. Flocking gives small birds like these some measure of protection from predators, and group effort makes finding food somewhat easier for all concerned.

Winding uphill, the trail traverses oak woods with a subcanopy of striped maple, a small but handsome tree with tight white-and-green-striped bark, and a shrub layer of blueberry and maple-leaf viburnum. Look closely at the oak trunks for signs of the alien gypsy moth. Hairy shed skins of gypsy moth caterpillars and brown, spindle-shaped pupal cases adhere to many oaks. Lacking natural enemies, this insect can defoliate large expanses of oak woodlands; the woodlands usually recover fully, however.

Soon you will arrive at the first vista, albeit screened by vegetation. In early October, when I made one of my visits here, the scarlet foliage of red maple and the yellow leaves of black birch were especially pleasing as the sun's rays passed through and illuminated them like shards of stained glass. To the west are power lines that carry electricity south from the power plant.

After crossing Rock Oak Ramble cart road, follow Rose Ledge Trail (also known as Mariah Trail) uphill. Here especially notice the thin, stacked layers that make up the gneiss bedrock. Brown and dry, leafy lichens cling tightly to the rocks and absorb moisture during rains, turning green. There is another partially screened view toward the west coming up; but more evocative are the views back down the trail as you ascend. Your attention may be diverted to something closer at hand—at five inches long, black-throated blue warblers move through the foliage in search of moth larvae and other insects. These lovely summer residents must fatten up for their long migration to the tropics. The female, in contrast to the strikingly attired male, is a nondescript brown with a bright white wing patch.

As you reach the sunny fringes of the crest, the views become truly spectacular to the west and north—Mt. Greylock in the Berkshires and Mt. Haystack in Vermont will be visible on a clear day. This is a fine spot for lunch and a great excuse—if you need one—to simply sit and enjoy the wonderful scenery. Such a perch is an ideal site, too, especially in fall, to scan for raptors—hawks, vultures, and ravens. A flock of seven ravens—doing a lot more gliding than crows would have—passed by, as did a Cooper's hawk. The rock of Rose Ledges has a pink hue and that perhaps is reason enough for this formation's name.

After leaving the vista point continue on Rose Ledge Trail past the Bump Ascutnee Trail junction on the right, which goes downhill. Many low, flat ledge outcrops are covered by the leafy lichens and surrounded by blueberry and oaks. Blueberries do well in the shallow, acidic soils and provide tasty berries for both wildlife and humans in August. Coarse bracken fern becomes more common as you proceed and wintergreen is abundant. The trail descends gradually, passing knee-high patches of light green sheep laurel. Although not nearly as imposing as its larger relative, mountain laurel, sheep laurel's smaller flowers—which also bloom in June—are a more intense pink. Laurels possess flowers with ingenious devices for depositing pollen on visiting insects. Spring-loaded stamens pop free, hitting the unwitting pollinator with a dose of pollen as it clambers about the blossom.

Upon reaching the Hill 'N' Dale cart road turn right. Soon reach the T intersection with 10th Mountain cart road, which is fairly level, wide, and manicured. Turn left and walk through oak woods to the intersection with Tooleybush Turnpike. Turn right and go uphill slightly to cross the paved Reservoir Road loop and walk to the observation platform overlooking the reservoir. Although this is the 1,100-foot summit of Northfield Mountain, the level plateau's setting belies the fact that you've climbed 817 vertical feet since leaving the visitor center. The southwestern end of the reservoir, its shores largely unvegetated, may host some waterfowl and perhaps other wildlife. Our best bird sighting here on the October trek was an American kestrel (formerly sparrow hawk), whose diet consists primarily of insects and mice.

To return, retrace your steps back down Rose Ledge Trail to Bump Ascutnee Trail on the left. Just before the junction are two tiny ponds on the left side of the cart road—these pools may support breeding salamanders and wood frogs in early spring. Proceed downhill on Bump Ascutnee Trail past outcrops of layered gneiss bedrock. Some of the ledges are between 15 and 25 feet in height. Pass an old quarry site, left, with a pit some 20 feet across; this, too, might be a vernal pool. As you continue along the trail, the ledges become more impressive—eventually reaching a height of 50 or 60 feet. We encountered quite a large group of young rock climbers literally being "taught the ropes" by older, more experienced instructors. We watched their efforts with some fascination. This location was apparently almost directly below where we had stopped for lunch atop the ledges.

From the trail are nice, partially screened views through the trees of the formidable layer cake rock wall. Fissured as it is with crevices, the outcroppings provide ideal denning sites for porcupines, which characteristically seek shelter in such locations. These plump rodents do not hibernate but instead gnaw the nutritious cambium or inner bark from trees during the winter months. Despised by some as destroyers of timber, shade, and fruit trees, porcupines are unabashedly one of my favorite woodland creatures—they pose little real threat to the vast forested landscape of western Massachusetts.

The trail parallels the cliffs for quite a distance. Cross Yellowjacket Pass cart road. The orange-blazed Lower Rose Ledge Trail descends through forest of oak and birch. Some of the red oaks are quite imposing. Pass into noticeably younger woodland of birch and maple, almost all the trees having a diameter of about seven inches—indicating a virtual clear-cut in the fairly recent past. A few very large trees were spared—perhaps to provide shade for livestock; one red oak's blackish trunk is all of three feet in diameter.

After descending most of the way, walk a little bit uphill and through a stand of young white pines, paralleling the power line cut you spied from above. The trail turns left and enters the cleared strip; the edge of the cut provides an opportunity for a mostly unobstructed view of wooded hills and cornfields. After a brief ramble in the sun, reenter the woods and pass through a hemlock stand where small flocks of three-and-one-half-inch-long golden-crowned kinglets search for minute insect prey in spring and fall. Males possess a central orange crown stripe whereas females sport a lemon yellow one. When you reach the junction with Rose Ledge Trail, turn left and follow it downhill back to the visitor center.

Getting There

Take I-91 north to Route 2 east (Exit 27) in Greenfield. Follow Route 2 east for 4.6 miles to Route 63. From the intersection of Routes 2 and 63, travel north on Route 63 for 5.3 miles to the paved entrance road on the right, just before a cemetery on the same side. Follow the entrance road for 0.15 mile to the large public parking area just northeast of the visitor center. Trails are open every day, except during mud season in March and early April (call the visitor center for exact dates).

The center is open 9:00 A.M. to 5:00 P.M., Wednesday through Sunday, April through November, and daily during winter for cross-country skiing. Contact the center for holiday schedule and hours at 413-659-3713.

No admission fees for hiking; there is a charge for cross-country skiing—rentals of skis and snowshoes available. Rest rooms on lower level of visitor center; pit toilet at trailhead. Picnic area located at visitor center. Public programs are conducted throughout the year and many require preregistration. Mountain biking (cart roads only—all bikers must register), rock climbing, orienteering, horseback riding, and hunting (except in no hunting zone in lower section of trail system) permitted. Dogs must be leashed at all times.

—R.L.

Erving State Forest
Erving/Warwick/Orange
4,479 acres

- 0.9 mile
- 1.5 hours
- easy

Imagine my surprise when I quite unexpectedly came upon a stunning view of Mt. Monadnock—its triangular mass rearing up stalwartly above the forested ridges. Even though more than 20 miles distant, the naked summit of this well-known peak seemed almost touchable.

The property possesses few bona fide hiking trails; a short, easy loop trail leads up a modest slope through a lovely hardwood forest with a shrub layer of thick mountain laurel and hobblebush. The views from an unnamed hilltop are very nice, and just beyond this vantage point, you emerge into a small clearing with the stunning beauty of Monadnock looming in the distance. Dense forests of birch, maple, oak, and hemlock cover the hills and valleys, and Laurel Lake provides an interesting contrast. A fascinating community of bog plants exists at the far west end of the lake where there is also an active beaver lodge that allows close inspection.

After parking at the large paved lot just beyond the contact station on Laurel Lake Road, walk back up past the contact station (approximately 35 feet) to the trail-head, left. Follow the path into the hemlock forest opposite the lake. Cross a bubbling brook on a small wooden roofed-over bridge. The woods are characteristically rocky with many moss-covered boulders. Three-inch-long two-lined salamanders spend the daylight hours safely beneath flat stones along the brook margins, while the more numerous red-backed salamander can be found under rotting logs in moist woods.

Beyond the hemlocks the character of the forest changes. Increased sunlight supports tiny forests of princess pine (only inches high) on the forest floor, thick-leaved bracken fern, and the ground-hugging light green leaves of trailing arbutus (also known as mayflower), the Massachusetts state flower. This species, with its white flowers and evergreen leaves, is quite common in the sunny margins along the path. A profusion of **mountain laurel** forms the understory. Its thick, shiny green leaves and white/pink flowers add pleasing color while blooming in early summer and in winter, when the ever-green leaves offset the stark grays and browns of the winter woods.

On the summit you'll find a few pitch pines. This tree often displays a picturesque appearance—gnarled and windblown. The stiff needles, in bundles of three, sometimes growing directly from the trunk, distin-guishing it from the more common white pine, which has five soft needles. Both grow on this exposed perch and combine to create a wonderful perfume. Rock-lov-ing common polypody fern caps some boulders, and fleshy evergreen marginal wood fern also favors these rocky sites. Silvery green reindeer moss and other slow-growing, persevering lichens have colonized the bare rock. There is also a small patch of sheep laurel (said to be poisonous to sheep) decidedly shorter than its larger relative. Linger for the views of oak woods to the south; this and the next vista point are perfect for snack or lunch breaks.

Watch for migrant hawks passing overhead in Sep-tember and October or perhaps a common raven. I always feel fortunate to see and hear one of these impressive big black birds. Fully four times the weight of the more familiar crow, ravens to me epitomize wildness. Their guttural croak speaks of vast, unbroken reaches of forest, steep cliffs, and rugged mountains. Absent from the commonwealth for some 100 years until 1983, ravens are again colonizing the maturing woodlands of western Massachusetts and I for one am thankful. The virtual clearing of the state's forests for agriculture eliminated or greatly reduced woodland species, including raven.

Continue on down the trail through more hardwoods, including clumps of American chestnut (once a dominant tree until the chestnut blight of the 1930s made the species all but extinct), to the aforementioned view of Mt. Monadnock, 22 miles away to the northeast (as the

Lying beyond miles of nearly unbroken forest, the pyramidal mass of Mt. Monadnock looms into view as you round a curve in the trail.

raven flies). Add some splendid fall foliage and you have the ingredients for wonderful photo opportunities. Behind you to the left is the broken cliff face, its outline softened by red maples and other plants.

To return to the parking lot and your car, continue on the gradually descending trail. In late summer and fall, the bright red berries of both creeping partridgeberry (small, paired, rounded leaves) and wintergreen (three leaves) dot the forest floor. Wintergreen contains a fragrant oil used for flavoring. White-breasted nuthatch and brown creeper diligently search bark crevices for insects and their eggs. Nuthatches generally descend trees while creepers ascend them. Eastern chipmunks scurry across the ground, sometimes giving a long series of high chirps that sound remarkably birdlike. Red squirrels, meanwhile, scamper from tree to tree recovering pinecones they've cut with their sharp incisors and caching the booty for later use. Both are hunted by coyotes—look for their hair- and bone-filled scat along the trail.

At the terminus of the trail, walk down steps with railings to Laurel Lake Road. Turn left and walk approximately 250 feet back to the parking area and your vehicle. You might want to explore briefly the shore of Laurel Lake and scan the surface for waterfowl before leaving. A number of privately owned cabins are situated along the opposite shoreline.

By driving west on Laurel Lake Road, back the way you came, you'll reach the public boat ramp in 0.6 mile on the right. You may wish to park here and walk the short distance to the west end of the lake, where the bog vegetation and beaver pond are located. Wetland shrubs including bright red-berried winterberry line this causeway. It's a native holly, which loses its leaves in fall. On the left, notice a medium-sized beaver lodge against the opposite shore. In fall the industrious rodents add large quantities of mud from the lake bottom to the structure, insulating it against the elements. I also saw a total of a dozen eastern painted turtles, our most common species, basking in the bright sunlight of an early October day here. They seemed to be soaking up sunlight before wintering at the bottom of the pond—their metabolic processes slowed to a point just adequate to sustain life.

A thick growth of sphagnum moss (the source of peat moss) borders the shoreline and the tiny islets. Bullhead lily leaves float on the surface, while the acid-soil shrubs **leatherleaf** and **sweetgale** grow in the developing bog—adding their decaying leaves to the mix. Within this moisture-rich yet nutrient-poor substrate thrive plants that have adapted by supplementing their diets with insects. **Pitcher plants**—almost otherworldly in their appearance—grow in clumps along the water's edge, trapping insects that wander down their open gullets. Stiff downward-pointing bristles and sweet secretions lead the bugs in but prevent their escape. Enzymes dissolve them and the plant absorbs the goodies. This is one of the most accessible places to see these fascinating plants.

Getting There

From the intersection of Route 2 (the Mohawk Trail) and North Street in Erving (if coming from the east); Church Street (if arriving from the west—look for a State Forest sign just before the fire station on the left), travel north on North Street (a right turn if coming from the east) to Swamp Road on the right. Turn onto Swamp Road, cross the brook, and follow the road northeast into the State Forest. It is 1.7 miles from Route 2 to the State Forest boundary. This road later becomes Laurel Lake Road, passes the entrance to the campground on the right, and in another 1.2 miles brings you to the contact station and parking area just beyond it on the left.

Hours are sunrise to sunset, unless you're camping. Parking fee is two dollars per vehicle. Roadside parking is prohibited. A modern brick rest room building (handicapped accessible) is located adjacent to the parking area and is open during the summer months. Swimming is allowed and changing houses are available. A pit toilet near the beach is also wheelchair accessible. Fishing is a popular activity on Laurel Lake.

—R.L.

Wendell State Forest

Wendell
7,557 acres

10/96
canoeing @
Wickett pond

- **1.4 miles**
- **2 hours**
- **easy**

The largest beaver lodge I have seen in Massachusetts sits near the western shore of Ruggles Pond in the southwestern portion of Wendell State Forest. It must be 20 feet across at the waterline and 8 feet high. The trail around the pond allows views from fairly close range. I did just that on an easy walk one bright early October day—taking several photos of the lodge with a backdrop of fiery red maple foliage.

After parking in the lot at the picnic area on the north side of the road (opposite the pond), cross the road and walk to steps leading up into another picnic area along the west shore of Ruggles Pond. Cathedral white pines tower above the picnic tables. Follow the trail through the picnic area and come to a pavilion and playing fields on the right. Continue left along the pond shore. Blue plastic markers on the trunks and more recent white-painted blazes mark the trail.

Notice that the margins of the pond are spongy—thick with **sphagnum moss** that can hold 50 times its own weight in water. You are standing, in effect, on a

Wendell State Forest

Lyons Brook

Jerusalem Rd.

M-M Trail

Wickett Pond Rd.

M-M Trail

N

¼ mile

M-M Trail

Chestnut Hill Rd.

P

Ruggles Pond

beaver dam

Loop Trail

waterlogged, floating mat of vegetation—a bog that will eventually increase its area concentrically until it covers the entire pond surface. Look closely to see a true bog plant—**American cranberry**—growing amid the sphagnum. Cranberry is a creeping plant with tiny oblong shiny green leaves. The fruits are small, red, and astringent—very high in vitamin C. Watch your footing. Don't tramp around too much in this fragile bog environment, lest you damage it.

The **massive beaver lodge** is now close at hand. Its shape is pyramidal and it must weigh tons. Perched on branches at one end of the lodge was a rascally looking female belted kingfisher in the process of swallowing a small silvery fish. Two grayish brown eastern phoebes occupied the opposite end. Through my binoculars, I watched as one phoebe opportunistically picked an insect out of a spiderweb on top of the lodge.

I imagined that inside the safety of their dark lodge, a beaver family rested. Perhaps two six-month-

An impressive beaver lodge sits along the western shore of Ruggles Pond.

old kits lay with bodies curled together, touching their mother. The kits and their 50-pound parents, as well as two older siblings born 18 months ago, shared the big lodge. Much of each day now was spent cutting saplings and larger trees—mostly maple and birch—to reinforce the lodge and augment the family's winter larder. Under the cover of darkness, small trees were quickly cut and dragged into the water where the nutritious inner bark was consumed. De-barked twigs were transported in the animal's mouth to strengthen the lodge walls, along with hundreds of pounds of rich black mud brought up from the pond bottom by the beaver's front paws. Other unpeeled branches would be floated and forcibly jammed into the pond bottom, there to remain available under the ice until hunger prompted their retrieval.

Returning to the trail, swing away from the water. On this higher ground grow red maple, red oak, and considerable sheep laurel. A bit farther along, the much larger mountain laurel becomes common and a few large gneiss boulders dot the woodland floor. White pine then joins the mix of tree species; a few are large size. On my visit, one fallen specimen—two-and-one-half-feet thick—had recently been cleared from the trail. The clean chain saw cut revealed 90 growth rings; the last 30 were tightly packed—probably owing to competition with surrounding trees in the maturing forest.

At the southwest end of the pond the trail skirts a shrub swamp where many trees had recently been cut by beavers. Follow the trail over a rocky area and then across a small stream that feeds Ruggles Pond—across the wet spots on bog bridges. This area was loaded with robins during my early October walk. Apparently the flock was feeding on the abundant winterberries and other foods to be had here. Go left when the trail splits. Cross a bog bridge and head toward the pond. To the left is a stand of white pines through whose swaying boughs the autumn winds blow to make that pleasant whooshing sound.

The trail skirts the shrub swamp again and here a big black cherry tree, cut all the way around by beavers, still stands upright—at least for the time being. Cross more bog bridges and a gurgling brook with two large fallen trees across it—a hemlock and an oak. In this wet, rocky area eastern hemlocks become more prevalent. Soon the trail nears the pond with nice views of the water to the left.

While I was here, the melancholy screams of a **red-shouldered hawk** came to my ears. These large raptors, which feed largely on reptiles and amphibians, are quite uncommon and found primarily in swamp habitats like this. A thick growth of two-foot-tall leatherleaf shrubs rings the pond margin. The thick leaves have undersides dotted with numerous tiny, cinnamon brown scales. A luxuriant growth of emergent aquatic vegetation fills the lake. The leaves of yellow pond lily and the smaller water shield float on the calm surface. Beavers love to eat the fleshy roots of water lilies and readily dig them up.

This is fine amphibian habitat, too. Green frogs, spring peepers, and red-spotted newts are present. Listen for the amusing and distinctive plucked banjo string call of the green frog emanating from the pond—especially in summer. Frogs have existed for 350 million years, but scientists have noticed dramatic worldwide population decreases over the past decade. Several theories have been put forth and many causes may yet be found to explain this phenomenon. Painted turtles bask on logs in the pond well into fall. Like other turtles, they come ashore in late spring or early summer to lay their eggs in sandy, well-drained soils. The leathery eggs, if not found by raccoons or other predators, usually hatch in late summer. Temperatures within the nest determine whether all the embryos will develop into males or females!

After leaving the shoreline, you'll move away from the pond and enter a hemlock/white pine grove. The soils are saturated here, and the shallow-rooted hemlocks are easily toppled by wind. Over time this creates a **pit and mound topography**—pits left where the root mass of a hemlock was torn from the earth and next to it a mound created by the now decomposed roots and the soil that was once held in their grasp.

Follow the trail onto higher ground, and cross a small knoll covered with hemlock and gray birch. Impish ruby crowned kinglets, which nest farther north, stop off here twice each year, spring and fall. Kinglets are somewhat hyperactive and travel in small flocks. The male's red topknot is seldom visible. Descend from the knoll and walk along a hillside of hemlock on the right The woods are again dotted with granitic gneiss boulders covered with leafy brown lichens commonly known as rock tripe.

Follow the path sharply to the left and cross over stones under which flows another stream feeding Ruggles Pond. Even though you won't see the water, the sound of it beneath the stones is easily heard. A low beaver dam has backed the water up on your left. The trail turns sharply left again and enters red maple/white pine forest. Fallen needles form a soft, thick, comfortable cushion for your feet. Walk the short path to the water's edge. Small red dragonflies and large green darners hunt for mosquitoes and other flying insects and bask on rocks and logs with gauzy wings extended.

The main trail continues through a grove of large white pines. Look out across the pond toward the far shore and the large beaver lodge. Log bridges cover some wet spots. The trail follows the shoreline fairly closely back through pine/oak woodland to the public beach. Check the sand here for tracks of raccoon, opossum, Canada goose, and other wildlife. The picnic area and parking are across the road.

There are many other scenic trails in Wendell State Forest, including a portion of Metacomet-Monadnock Trail (blazed with white rectangles). One very nice walk of about two miles takes you from the same parking area north and downhill along beautiful, cascading Lyons Brook. It then swings right, through attractive forest of northern hardwoods to Jerusalem Road. Across this road stands an imposing sheer cliff. From there follow the road south and west back to your car—turn right at the intersection with Wickett Pond Road. Unfortunately, some trails are not well marked or maintained.

Getting There

From Route 2 in Greenfield, drive 10.0 miles east and cross the Connecticut River over the French King Bridge. Continue east (south) on Route 2 for 1.0 mile to

Route 63 in Millers Falls. Turn right onto Route 63 and follow it west and south across the Millers River for 0.7 mile. Turn right at the intersection (still Route 63) and drive west for 0.1 mile to where Route 63 bears left. Continue south for 0.3 mile on Route 63 to Highland Avenue on the left. Follow Highland Avenue for 0.5 mile to Wendell Road and turn right (a bridge that is out here necessitates this somewhat circuitous route). Follow Wendell Road for 3.1 miles to Chestnut Hill Road and turn left (forest headquarters are on your left). From the State Forest entrance, drive 0.3 mile to the picnic area and parking on the left.

Hours are 10:00 A.M.–4:00 P.M. weekdays, 10:00 A.M.–5:30 P.M. weekends. No admission fee. Pit toilets and drinking water are available at picnic area. Horses, bicycles, and snowmobiles are allowed on unpaved roads. Hunting is prohibited.

—R.L.

Mt. Sugarloaf
State Reservation
South Deerfield
532 acres

- **2.2 miles**
- **1.5 hours**
- **difficult (steep)**

Lying parallel to the west bank of the Connecticut River at the southern terminus of the Pocumtuck Ridge is South Sugarloaf Mountain—a sandstone hill accessible both by automobile and on foot. The rust-colored mound lies along Route 116, only one mile east of I-91. Most visitors drive to the summit to enjoy the fine views of the broad Connecticut Valley and the Mt. Tom and Holyoke Ranges, but the short (and in places steep) ascent on foot makes the vistas far more rewarding. True, the top is developed with paved parking, picnic area and pavilion, and a multilevel observation building with modern rest room facilities, but these creature comforts may seem a just reward for the exertion of the steep hike. For a short hike to a great view, Mt. Sugarloaf State Reservation is hard to beat.

Aptly named, South Sugarloaf is composed of **tightly cemented sand** (quartz grains) **and pebbles** and shaped roughly like a loaf of bread (oddly, it was never glaciated). South Sugarloaf stands 652 feet above sea

Mt. Sugarloaf State Reservation

avoid loop

N

steps

500 feet

Mountain Rd.

corn fields

very steep

Pocumtuck Ridge Trail

athletic field

South Sugarloaf Mtn.

P

MAIN
ENTRANCE

Route 116

power lines

level, not enough to make your ears pop but certainly a
fine perch from which to survey the countryside.

From the dusty parking lot, follow the path (red and
blue blazes) beneath the large spruce tree to the power

line right-of-way. Skirt the cornfield on the left and reenter the woods later, on the right. Cornfields, although a monoculture, can be productive wildlife-viewing areas after harvest. Be on the lookout—especially early and late in the day—for wild turkey, Canada geese, and deer. Even during midday, mourning dove and crow should be present. If the ground is wet or snow covered, look for telltale tracks leading from the shelter of the woods to the bounty of the cornfield.

The trail reenters the forest to the right and meets the woods road extension of Mountain Road. Turn right here and begin a gradual ascent through woods of birch and beech. The larger and higher mass of North Sugarloaf looms nearby on the left. Some of the black birches and oaks are quite large. Sadly, sprouts and small trees are all that is left of **American chestnut,** a former dominant in these woodlands. The tree was all but eradicated by the chestnut blight in the 1930s. Chestnut leaves resemble those of beech but are much longer and more strongly toothed. A fungus attacks the plumbing system of nearly all of today's chestnuts before they can mature and flower, and thus regeneration of this once noble tree is limited to sprouting from old stumps. Hay-scented, Christmas, and evergreen wood fern constitute an attractive green layer between the shrubs. Pass a small granite boundary marker, left.

When the trail splits, a short distance farther, follow the path on the right (red blazes) in a southerly direction toward the auto road and the summit. Ascend for about 200 yards and then reach a series of steps to a hairpin curve in the summit road. Stay left and walk along the road to where it forks. Enter the one-way (down only) portion of the road—the left fork. The blue-blazed Pocumtuck Ridge Trail begins on the left and ascends the hill very steeply. This east slope is quite precipitous and should only be attempted when trail conditions are dry—do not descend by this path, however, as it is quite dangerous! Even the way up requires you to hold on to small trees. You may wish instead simply to walk up the steep but paved road to the top (about 0.25 mile). You can then rejoin the trail on the right side of the road, opposite a paved parking area on the left.

If you do take the trail you may be too preoccupied with maintaining your footing and handholds to survey the bucolic Connecticut River floodplain scene, close at hand through the trees. Take the blue-blazed left fork at the top of the hill and cross the road again at the lower parking area. From here it is just a short distance to the summit. Pick up the trail on the right side of the road; here it is not marked. The path curves right and goes downhill to an overlook just above the auto road. From here enjoy gorgeous views of the farm fields and a row of tobacco barns in the fertile floodplain just below to the north and west. Reindeer moss and leathery common polypody fern fronds soften the basaltic rock outcrops at your feet. Tiny cow-wheat plants are abundant though easy to overlook, as their yellowish funnel-shaped flowers are anything but conspicuous.

From here it's just a few steps to the picnic area on the summit—the perfect place for lunch or a snack. The observation building has three levels, each affording a slightly better view to the south of the broad, winding Connecticut River, Amherst and the University of Massachusetts campus, and the Holyoke and Mt. Tom Ranges

Wooded ridges rise beyond the fertile fields and settlements of the Connecticut River Valley as you gaze westward.

in their entirety in the far distance. You may even be able to make out the summit house on Mt. Holyoke, 16 miles away (see p. 215) If the day is a sunny one in September or early October, watch for butterflies, including southbound monarchs; and, of course, keep a lookout for migrant hawks.

Wander about the summit and notice that red and white oaks and red and white pines dominate the top of South Sugarloaf. Maple-leaf viburnum, a shrub of low stature that produces blue-black berries in late summer as well as beautiful pink-purple foliage, can be seen, too. Smooth false foxglove, a lovely tall plant that flowers yellow in late summer and early fall, also grows in the sandy soil.

To return to your vehicle, it is best to follow the same route—with the notable exception of the extremely precarious portion east of the road. Carefully follow the access road instead, until you reach the steps leading down through the forest to the woods road and turn left (west). Turn left again upon reaching the trail parallel to the utility right-of-way.

For a wonderful view of the steep east face of South Sugarloaf, drive to the intersection of Route 116 and River Road (no parking here) on the west bank of the river where the Sunderland Bridge crosses the Connecticut. The sheer, rust-colored cliff face topped by the observation building is dramatically visible from there.

Getting There

From I-91 northbound, take Exit 24 (South Deerfield) and travel 1.2 miles east on Route 116 to an intersection just before the main entrance to the reservation (on your left). Turn left, pass the main entrance (auto road to the summit), and turn right, instead, into a dirt parking area.

Hours are sunrise to sunset. No admission fee. Auto road gates are locked at sunset. Horseback riding is allowed on woods roads. Motorized vehicles are prohibited except on paved road. Rest rooms are located at the south end of observation building.

—R.L.

High Ledges
Wildlife Sanctuary
Shelburne
570 acres

4/20/97

- **1.7 miles**
- **2.5 hours**
- **moderate**

Perched atop an exposed outcrop 1,000 feet above the scenic Deerfield River valley, High Ledges Wildlife Sanctuary on Massaemett Mountain offers magnificent views and wonderful wildlife observation opportunities. On a clear day you can see the state's highest peak, Mt. Greylock, 25 miles to the west. Rocky woodlands of oak, birch, maple, and hemlock clothe the broad, mostly level summit. Old fields, bordered by stone walls, brooks, and active beaver ponds add variety and interest to this picturesque and biologically diverse property. Established through land gifts to the Massachusetts Audubon Society in 1970 and 1976, the society continues to own and manage the property as an unstaffed sanctuary open to the public. Three additional parcels were added in the early 1990s, bringing the total acreage to 570.

The sanctuary's trail system is fairly extensive and quite well maintained, and enables the visitor to enjoy the full variety of fascinating natural community types present. A map and compass are helpful, however. The

High Ledges Wildlife Sanctuary

recommended loop trail described below encompasses Lady-slipper and Waterthrush Trails. This loop will take you through a wide variety of habitats, including open fields, sunny ledges, birch groves, and an orchid swamp.

After stopping in the informal grassy parking area at the terminus of the entrance road, take a few minutes to explore the lovely open fields. On a sunny summer day butterflies are common (I noted tiger swallowtail, spring azure, monarch, inornate ringlet, and pearl crescent, to name a few), and bluebirds and tree swallows nest (May through August) in the wooden nesting boxes. **Eastern bluebirds,** so beloved by many people, have made a heartening comeback over the past several decades, thanks in part to the installation of nest boxes like these. In this part of its range, the beautiful sky blue, brick orange, and white male and his duller mate usually raise two broods of three to five young over the course of the breeding season.

To begin, proceed north around the gate and follow the road through a meadow regenerating to red maple, black cherry, and white birch. These pioneering species need large amounts of sunlight to prosper. Meadowsweet, lowbush blueberry, and thorny red and black raspberry canes—studded with white flowers in late spring and early summer—fill the area. Lichen-covered stone walls mark old pasture boundaries as you walk gradually downhill to a small **vernal pool** on your left, just off the road. The pool's water may be thick with the little black tadpoles of wood frogs. Vernal pools such as this are essential for the breeding success of wood frogs and Jefferson and spotted salamanders. Indeed, these creatures can breed nowhere else, and a primordial spectacle is played out each spring as the first rains bring the creatures out of their winter dormancy and urge them on to this, their ancestral breeding pool.

Return to the road and continue walking northwestward, this time uphill. Soon a cottage on the ledges will come into view. Flaky-barked red pines grow on the **promontory of bare rock** to the left of the building. Settle down here for at least a few minutes to drink in the sublime panorama. Use caution as the drop-off is abrupt and there are no railings to safeguard you! The town of Shelburne Falls lies close at hand, southwest on the banks of the Deerfield River, a major tributary of the Connecticut. Most of what you'll see between here and Mt. Greylock (elevation 3,491 feet) is covered in forest of varying shades of green. The 1989 landslide on Greylock's east face is clearly visible, even without binoculars. Listen for the evocative, flutelike songs of hermit thrushes and the sweet trill of the gray (above) and white (below) dark-eyed junco. The latter, usually more a bird of northern forests, apparently finds the 1,450-foot elevation and climate here to its liking.

Continue walking northward along the escarpment through thick growths of shiny-leaved mountain laurel that harbor the well-concealed nests of black-throated blue warblers to the beginning of Lady-slipper Trail. Blue disks on tree trunks mark the trail (yellow disks on the opposite side of the trees signify that you are returning toward the trailhead). After a short distance heading downhill on a moderately steep trail, come to a four-way intersection. North Trail goes left, and Spring Brook Trail (red blazes) goes right. Continue straight on Lady-slip-

Mt. Greylock, the state's highest peak, is visible through red pine boughs from the ledges, 1,000 feet above the Deerfield River.

per Trail across Spring Brook. Trail maps are affixed to tree trunks at most trail intersections, and small signboards on the trees will also help you find your way.

On the right is a small mammal live-trapping grid, the second of three located on the property. They are part of ongoing field studies designed to shed more light on the abundance and diversity of small mammals at High Ledges. The results of this and other research are used by the society to craft an ecological management plan that will safeguard the interesting and sensitive natural communities while also allowing nonconsumptive use of the sanctuary by the public. One of the creatures found by using this technique was the big-eyed, nocturnal southern flying squirrel—not an animal that you are likely to see during a daytime ramble.

Follow the trail eastward past the junction with Wolves' Den Trail (left), cross another brook, and junction left with Gentian Swamp Trail. Here Lady-slipper Trail turns sharply south, right. Wonderful displays of **wildflowers** are one of the highlights of High Ledges. In late spring watch for the blossoms of red columbine—whose drooping bells have five curved spurs—Canada mayflower, false Solomon's seal, and wild ginger, which hides its ill-scented liver red flowers under the leaf litter where beetles are sure to find and pollinate them. As you continue along, summer birdsong, scampering eastern chipmunks, and red squirrels will lead you to the intersection with Waterthrush Trail at a damp, fern-covered spot. Among the nesting woodland birds you may see and hear along the way are the ovenbird (its loud "teacher, teacher, teacher" refrain is unmistakable) and the great crested flycatcher (a cavity nester with a yellow breast and rusty tail). In the wetland pockets look for

Canada warbler, common yellowthroat (the male has a black mask), and chestnut-sided warbler.

Turn left onto Waterthrush Trail and follow it downstream along Spring Brook in an easterly direction to an orchid swamp, on the left, where the trail turns abruptly right (southward). Golden ragwort is a tall composite with flowers the color of egg yolks. It favors wet ground, and you'll find it blooming here in late spring and early summer. Continue south along the edge of the swamp, emerging into the sunny fields that red foxes and deer frequent at twilight; turn right at the entry road and follow it for a distance of about 1,000 feet back to the trailhead and your vehicle.

Getting There

From the Greenfield rotary on Route 2 (also known as the Mohawk Trail), travel west for 5.4 miles into Shelburne and Little Mohawk Road on the right. Look for the tall white church steeple ahead on the right; watch also for signs to Davenport Maple Farm/Springbrook Campground. Turn right (north) onto Little Mohawk Road and follow it for 1.3 miles, turning left onto Patten Road (no sign). Follow Patten Road for just over 1.1 miles to Square Lot Road on the left where a small sign for the sanctuary is located. Note the stone wall to the right of the drive. Follow the dirt road for 0.4 mile to the parking area and trailhead just short of the metal gate.

Hours are dawn to dusk; closed from late fall (including deer hunting season) to late spring, as the gravel road becomes impassable. Limited parking. No rest rooms. Picking of flowers or fruit is strictly prohibited.

—R.L.

Bear Swamp Reservation

Ashfield
213 acres ①MARCH 22
1997
②12/20/97

- 2.5 miles
- 2.5 hours
- moderate

The rocky woodlands of Bear Swamp Reservation shelter seemingly incongruous stone walls or, more accurately, stone fences—built some 150 years ago by farmers to mark property lines and confine livestock. This attractive, little-visited property is blessed with an abundance of spring wildflowers as well as a wide range of wildlife. It beckons nature lovers to spend a few hours, or a whole day, enjoying nature's diversity.

You'll follow mostly well-marked trails through rich woodlands that are home to tiny short-tailed shrews, coyotes, and black-throated blue warblers; across fast-flowing brooks; past lichen-covered ledges and outcrops where porcupines find safe haven; and along beaver ponds hosting mink, dragonflies, red-spotted newts, painted turtles, and tree swallows. From Beaver Brook Trail you'll get a fairly close look at a small, active beaver lodge.

Lying for the most part above 1,500 feet, this property is defined by north-south trending ridges of metamorphic rock, hundreds of millions of years old. More

Bear Swamp Reservation

recently it was sculpted by ice, too. Alternating with the rocky folds are wet pockets—shrub swamps, beaver ponds, and ephemeral vernal pools. The cool, moist climate has favored the vigorous growth of northern hardwoods—birch, beech, and maple, as well as hemlock on the north-facing slopes and ravines. Red spruce, a boreal tree, imparts a somewhat wild, northern feel to the place.

The loop combination of Beaver Brook Trail to Fern Glade Trail to Bear Swamp Road to North-South Trail and finally to Lookout Trail will enable you to traverse communities from shrub swamps to forested ravines. These trails climb and descend several modest ridges with lookouts to the pond, cross babbling brooks, skirt a shrub swamp filled with lovely cinnamon ferns, and return to the beaver pond shore.

After parking off Hawley Road, proceed up Beaver Brook Trail and into the forest, past posts designed to deny entry to motor vehicles. The rather wide path (marked with painted white triangles and round green plastic disks) leads up through eastern hemlocks, yellow birch, American beech, sugar maple, black birch, and moisture-tolerant white ash. Indian cucumber-root, creeping partridgeberry, false Solomon's seal, and wild sarsaparilla are the most abundant flowering herbs. You will also see heart-leaved hobblebush and shiny leaved, evergreen mountain laurel. Shortly, the trail crosses a small stream. Follow the trail to the left (this is the junction of Beaver Brook and Lookout Trails.) You'll later return to this spot as you follow Lookout Trail back to close the loop.

Beaver Brook Trail passes stone walls to the right (just before crossing the pond's rock-lined outlet stream) and soon reaches the beaver pond—also on the right. A slight detour takes you to the shore where, around to the right, you'll be able to glimpse an active beaver lodge situated along the edge of a small rocky island dotted with

red spruce. Watch for leopard frogs, red-spotted newts, and green frogs that often announce their presence with a loud shriek when startled. While relaxing here one June day I saw a huge great horned owl fly silently from its exposed perch into the seclusion of the bordering woodland. This, our biggest owl, feeds on large prey—rabbits, grouse, and even skunks.

Return to the main trail and continue right (south) along the eastern edge of the pond. A few hundred yards beyond the pond outflow, turn left onto Fern Glade Trail, blazed with blue crescents (Beaver Brook Trail continues toward the right around the pond). Mountain laurel is abundant here. Laurel produces clusters of showy white and pink nickel-sized blossoms where it receives enough sunlight in late June and early July. A bit farther on, large yellow birches with fine peeling brassy bark and red maples predominate.

The trail passes an isolated vernal pool, on the right, where spotted and Jefferson salamanders and wood frogs breed. Cross a little, fast-flowing brook and head uphill through a small, darkened hemlock gorge where little is able to grow on the forest floor. Tiny, loudly singing winter wrens favor such moist, rocky ravines. After leveling out, the trail passes through young beech forest to another woodland pool, on the left. Vernal pools are vital to the reproductive success of several species of amphibians, since they can only carry out early spring courtship, mating, and egg laying in such ephemeral waters. In summer, its most easily seen inhabitants are the small black tadpoles of wood frogs.

Fern Glade Trail continues southerly in a nearly straight line over fairly level ground through broadleaf woodland. In spring, look for red trillium (three petals) and sessile-leaved bellwort (a lily). The trail reaches Bear Swamp Road (paved). Along the road's sunlit edges, watch for eye-catching black and yellow tiger swallowtail butterflies feeding on orange hawkweed and striking **black damselflies** fluttering near flowing water—the males have brilliant neon blue abdomens!

Turn right onto the road and walk west less than 0.1 mile. Reenter the moist woodland on the right where North-South Trail is marked by a sign. Cross a small brook near the road and head north along the stream. Trail blazes here are blue bands around the trunks of small trees. Soon pass an extensive swamp, left, with a luxuriant growth of cinnamon fern—so-called because its

A black-and-yellow tiger swallowtail probes for nectar on an orange hawkweed along the sunny shoulders of Bear Swamp Road.

fertile fronds are an attractive orange-tan. These woods shelter an array of wood warblers: black-throated green in white pines, black-throated blue in laurel and hobble-bush thickets, and black and white warbler creeping along the branches of maples like a nuthatch. Beautiful Canada warblers nest in cool, moist situations like this.

Beyond the swamp, the trail passes through wood-land dominated by beech, northern red oak, birch, and black cherry (identified by its flaky blackish bark). Soon you're heading gradually downhill to cross a stone wall. Eastern chipmunks are the most noticeable daytime mammals in these woods. In fall they're busy caching acorns and other goodies under logs and in hollows for the coming winter. The trail then makes brief east and north jogs and descends to a lovely cascading brook. North-South Trail blazes are blue arrows above a horizontal blue band.

About one-half hour after leaving Bear Swamp Road, you'll reach a trail junction. Turn right onto Beaver Brook Trail, marked by white triangles above a blue line, and continue downstream. At the site of an **enormous hemlock** the trail swings right, southeast. You'll see another beaver pond to the left and then reach and cross another stone wall. Follow a moss-covered ledge on the right and then cross a spring-fed brook.

At the intersection of Beaver Brook and Lookout Trails, turn abruptly left onto Lookout Trail over rock outcroppings and climb gradually to lichen-covered boulders, on the right. At the second intersection turn right and walk up through a crevice to reach a sunny ledge overlooking the beaver pond. Reenter the shaded forest of beech, black birch (smooth black bark), and hemlock by walking to the left. Here the ethereal sounds of hermit thrushes float through the air on late spring and summer evenings. Crow-sized pileated woodpeckers are quite common. Look for their large, deep rectangular excavations—a sign that one of these red-crested birds has discovered and feasted upon a carpenter ant colony. The trail then follows along the base of a large ledge, right, and turns to the right. Note the **huge American beech** on your left. Beechnuts are much favored by wild turkeys, blue jays, squirrels, chipmunks, deer, and other furred and feathered creatures.

Enter a maple/ash woods and go quite steeply downhill. The trail eventually becomes narrow, swings to the right, and follows along the edge of a small gorge. Here it is not well marked. Walk down along a rocky slope, with small cliffs to the right. Continue to within sight of the beaver pond and then curve left. This will take you to the pond, where the trail turns left again to roughly follow the shoreline east. A short informal spur trail on the right will take you to the water's edge. Look for beaver signs—branches stripped of their bark and marked by the rodents' sharp, ever-growing incisor teeth—floating in the water. In the shrubby wetlands nest alder flycatcher (whose breeding song is "fee-bee-o"), common yellowthroat, and lovely chestnut-sided warbler. Continue on the main trail past rock outcrops to the brook joining the trail. Continue left to return you to your car.

For a short easy walk of 0.7 mile round-trip to an excellent overlook of Apple Valley, cross Hawley Road, walk left (north) about 150 feet beyond the reservation sign, and follow the wide four-wheel-drive track to the left up through hemlock woods. Where the road splits, stay right and proceed uphill. Soon you'll break out into a sunny clearing. The trail swings to the right and takes you to the top of a bedrock outcrop. Here a plaque commemorates the gift of this property by Mr. and Mrs. Steinmetz. To your left the view extends beyond Apple Valley and all the way to Vermont. In fall, the brilliant golden foliage and bright white trunks of paper birch make for splendid photographic opportunities.

Getting There

From the intersection of I-91 and Route 116 in Deerfield, take Route 116 west for nearly 11.0 miles through the towns of Deerfield, Conway, and Ashfield to Ashfield center. Approximately 0.9 mile west of Ashfield center, Route 116 junctions with Route 112 to form combined (briefly) Routes 116/112. Travel straight across Routes 116/112 onto paved Hawley Road and drive 1.7 miles to the reservation entrance on the left—look for the sign (you'll pass Bear Swamp Road on the left at the 0.9-mile mark, but continue straight on Hawley Road for another 0.8 mile).

Open sunrise to sunset. No admission fee. Parking along both sides of the road is limited. No rest rooms. Cross-country skiing is permitted. Camping, fires, and motorized vehicles are prohibited.

—R.L.

Chapelbrook Reservation
South Ashfield
143 acres

- **along Chapel Brook, 0.75 mile**
- **30 minutes**
- **easy**
- **Pony Mountain, 1.0 mile**
- **45 minutes**
- **medium**
- **great for children**

Small brook trout dart for cover in the aquamarine-colored pool. The sound of **falling water** is all around as the mountain stream known as Chapel Brook drops over a series of ledges. The first falls are 10 feet high, the next are 15, and then finally the stream tumbles 25 feet before continuing through a dark wood of hemlock. What a wonderful place to soak up the combination of woods and water! Chapel Brook is nestled in the foothills that ascend to the Berkshires near Route 9 climbing above the Connecticut Valley, also known as the Pioneer Valley.

The hiking here is terrific—one trail follows the stream while a second ascends nearby Pony Mountain. From the small parking area on Williamsburg Road, most visitors prefer to view the falls next to the road and then follow an old woodland road that parallels the stream in a downhill direction. Old stone walls and

Chapelbrook Reservation

Williamsburg Road

N

1000 feet

Pony
Mountain

roof
area

main
face
(ledge)

Summit Trail

Chapel Brook

P

stone
foundation

wildflowers are scattered beneath a canopy of large deciduous and evergreen trees. In the spring, look for pink lady's slippers and the delicate white flower of trillium. (The lady's slipper flower is a veined pouch, and it has two oval leaves at the base. The trillium has three broad leaves and three showy petals.) Deer use the trail between dawn and dusk—watch for their pointed hoofprints in the sand.

After about a 10-minute walk, you will notice that the stream flows closer to the trail and the rushing sound of water is your companion again. Look for the stone

A wide trail at Chapelbrook leads through a forest of maple and birch.

remains of what appears to be an old mill. With a little imagination you can picture horses hauling lumber or corn along this old road to an active little mill that used the stream as its power. The trail ends at private property, and you should retrace your steps back to the parking area.

The climb up Pony Mountain begins on the other side of Williamsburg Road and takes about 45 minutes round-trip. The trailhead is opposite the falls near a Trustees of Reservations sign on the north side of the stream. Follow the main trail, called the Summit Trail, as it first leads around the base of the mountain and begins a gradual climb that brings you to the summit. Although the trail is steep in spots, the sight of impressive **cliffs** near the summit can give you the energy to push on. On my hike I heard the unmistakable sound of a ruffed grouse drumming its wings—first slowly, then building rapidly before its abrupt end. I never saw the grouse, but two ravens were perched at the top of a nearby tree calling out an eerie three-note "awk, awk, awk."

The forlorn cries of the raven made me think about another creature that is officially nonexistent here in Massachusetts—the mountain lion. If the state does have mountain lions, this is the kind of remote, hilly region where they just might roam undetected. Over the years, there have been plenty of mountain lion sightings in the Berkshires but no conclusive proof. Yet there are plenty of bears around, and in all my years of hiking I have seen only one. If bears can stay well hidden, is it possible that a few mountain lions have avoided humans altogether? (The mountain lion has a long tail and yellow-brown fur, and its chest and throat are white. Females average 100 pounds and males average 150. Not including the two- to three-foot tail, a male mountain lion can measure almost eight feet long!)

On your way to the summit, pass through a beautiful beech grove. Their smooth gray trunks are a pleasure to behold, especially in autumn when their yellow leaves blanket the forest floor. Near the ridge top is an open field—it is private property but you can scan the edges of this open land for deer. Other creatures that live here but are rarely seen are coyote, barred owls, and the magnificent pileated woodpecker.

The trail passes through dense stands of hemlock as it turns to a southerly direction along the ridge top. Occasionally there are sections of exposed granite visible. Your pace will quicken when you see open sky ahead through the trees, signifying that you are near the summit. Spectacular views to the south, overlooking the quiet valley, await your arrival. Look down on a farm and tiny black dots of cows and horses in open fields. In the fall, enjoy a kaleidoscope of color, particularly from the treetops that are directly in front of the cliff. Sit here and rest to the murmur of the wind whispering through the evergreens before retracing your steps back to your car and civilization.

Getting There

From Ashfield center take Route 116 east 1.5 miles to South Ashfield. Where Route 116 turns left, continue straight ahead on Williamsburg Road (follow Williamsburg Road Route 9 signs) 2.2 miles. Entrance is on the right at the bridge.

Open year-round, seven days a week, no admission fee, no rest rooms.

—M.T.

D.A.R. State Forest

Goshen/Ashfield
1,536 acres

10/96

- 2.5 miles
- 2.5 hours
- moderate

Possessing great wildlife diversity, extensive northern hardwood forest, swamps, lakes, and ponds, D.A.R. State Forest is a wonderful place for a day of walking, nature study, and panoramic vistas. Because most of the area lies above 1,400 feet elevation, the growing season is curtailed; this has a profound influence on the plants and animals that live here. Stands of red spruce, bunchberry, and boggy pockets give clues to the northern character of this forest. A lookout tower on high Moore Hill (1,697 feet) rewards you with a magnificent 360-degree view of the surrounding wooded ridges, including the nearby Chapelbrook Ledges (see p. 158).

Unmistakable evidence of earlier agriculture stands in the form of rock walls and old cellar holes, found in this maturing beech/maple/hemlock woodland. The Massachusetts chapter of the Daughters of the American Revolution donated the property to the state in 1929. In the 1930s, the Civilian Conservation Corps (CCC) built roads, buildings, and other facilities that remain in use today. A fairly extensive network of well-maintained

D.A.R. State Forest

N

500 feet

Twining Brook Pond

hemlock grove

Long Trail

Darling Trail

observation tower

P

private beach

Nature Center

Moore Hill Rd.

Oak Hill Rd.

beach

Route 112

Upper Highland Lake

beach

P

P

and easy-to-follow (with a few exceptions) trails and dirt roads allows you to explore virtually every corner of this scenic forest. The walking is quite easy and the few hills are moderate.

Woodlands and wetlands shelter **black bear** (campers are advised to lock away their food) and bobcat, as well as the less glamorous but far more numerous red eft, a terrestrial salamander that becomes the aquatic red-spotted newt later in life. Signs of beaver and white-tailed deer are quite common along the wetland margins. Among breeding birds is the uncommon **Swainson's thrush,** as well as a dozen or more species of **wood warblers,** including black-throated blue, black-throated green, magnolia, and northern waterthrush (I found 33 species of birds on one early July visit). Pink lady's slipper orchids, painted and red trilliums, Canada mayflower, and clintonia (a.k.a. blue-bead lily) brighten the woodlands in spring.

Your walk will take you from hemlock and laurel-fringed Twinning Brook Pond on Long Trail, through woodland and wetland, to the eastern shore of lovely Upper Highland Lake, and then to the summit of Moore Hill.

To reach the trailhead follow the paved loop road through the group campground (stay right) to Twinning Brook Pond on the right. Park and follow the Long Trail near the northeast end of the pond, closest to the campground, with an Area Closed (to camping) sign. Almost immediately cross Twinning Brook on a small wooden bridge. In early July, I was delighted to find a nest containing three large-mouthed, nestling robins in an arrowwood shrub near the pond's edge. The middle nestling, its head topped by a tuft of gray down, watched me through half-opened eyelids. The parent birds voiced their concern at my untimely arrival, so after a couple of quick photos I left the adults to the demanding business of rearing their hungry offspring.

Continue southwesterly past the pond and up a gradual incline as it roughly parallels a small brook. After approximately 0.3 mile, you'll reach a trail junction. Follow the Long Trail right and walk a short distance to another junction. A left turn would take you to the Darling Trail. Instead, continue on the Long Trail by turning right. The trail traverses beech woods. There is rocky ledge to the left. After approximately 1,000 feet, the trail makes a broad swing left and begins gradually to descend. Pass through a dark hemlock grove and a swampy area on log bridges and reach an intersection. Goldthread adds a bit of color to the dark, rather bare forest floor with its bright green leaves and white flowers. (Goldthread's name refers to the color of its roots.)

At the trail junction, where a sign reads 0.25 mile to Campground, turn right—away from the campground—to continue on Long Trail. The trail makes another broad bend and proceeds gently down through wet hemlock woods and crosses a brook just before reaching the northern end of Upper Highland Lake. Note a No Trespassing sign on the right indicating the forest boundary. After reaching the lake (elevation 1,427 feet), the trail heads south along the eastern shore. From gaps in the thick shoreline vegetation, notice two beaver lodges—one on the far shore, the other on the near side of a small peninsula. A private camp is visible on the opposite shore.

Boating and fishing are popular activities. I saw fish jumping while I relaxed along the picturesque shoreline. You may wish to linger here awhile yourself. Notice the bur reed growing in the shallows. Its spiky round flowers look like miniature medieval maces.

To continue, walk southerly on Long Trail to the Darling Trail junction, left. A sign here reads Campground 0.25 mile. Follow the Darling Trail away from the lake, proceeding gradually uphill. Listen for hermit thrush, veery, and little brown creeper, which creeps up

A watchful robin nestling eyes an intruder from its nest in an arrowwood shrub.

tree trunks. The creeper's decurved, forcepslike bill is perfectly designed for removing insects, spiders, and their eggs from bark crevices.

Approach the paved campground road and notice the modern rest room building with a drinking fountain outside. Follow the paved road straight ahead through the campground and pick up the Darling Trail again, just left of another drinking fountain at campsite #49 R. The Darling Trail has no markers but is easy to find and follow. Scarlet tanager (the female is green), yellow-bellied sapsucker, solitary and red-eyed vireos all nest in these woods.

After passing through beech/maple forest with an understory of mountain laurel, the trail leads uphill to a power line cut. Just after leaving the woods, spot an old cellar hole to the left of the trail. Follow the power line path about 200 yards to Moore Hill Road. The artificial "edge" habitat of the power line cut enables gray catbird, chestnut-sided warbler, and many butterflies to find suitable conditions. It also allows female brown-headed cowbirds access to the nests of interior woodland birds; the cowbird (a brood parasite) lays its eggs in the nest of another, generally smaller species.

Cross Moore Hill Road and follow the hiking/bridle trail immediately opposite up the slope to the observation tower, surrounded by tall trees including some sizable white pines. Climb the steps of the metal tower to obtain good views. Green ridges roll on into the distance with few signs of human habitation. Two miles away to the northeast, as the crow flies, sit the bare rock Chapelbrook Ledges—a small light-colored island surrounded by a sea of green. On a really clear day distant views of Mt. Greylock (northwest), the Holyoke and Mt. Tom Ranges (southeast), and even New Hampshire's Mt. Monadnock (northeast) are possible.

After taking in the stunning vistas, descend and walk to the back of the tower (opposite the steps). An unmarked, and at first not easily apparent, trail descends to Moore Hill Road, crossing dirt Oak Hill Road in the process. Pick up the trail just slightly to the left after crossing the dirt road. After reaching paved Moore Hill Road, turn right and walk slightly downhill approximately 0.25 mile to a trail, left, leading back to Twinning Brook Pond (stay right at the last junction) and the group campground where you left your vehicle.

Getting There

From the intersection of Routes 9 and 112 in Goshen, travel north on Route 112 for 0.7 mile to the well-marked State Forest entrance road on the right. Follow the entrance road (Moore Hill Road) to the visitor contact station where fees are collected. A large parking lot on the left accommodates the many summer visitors. To reach the trailhead at the group camping area, continue on Moore Hill Road for 1.6 miles and turn left onto the group camp loop road. Moore Hill Road is usually gated beyond the group camp turnoff.

Hours are dawn to dusk, unless you're camping. Entry fee is two dollars per car. Rest rooms are available but not at the group campground. Camping, picnicking, swimming, boating, fishing, horseback riding, snowmobiling, and cross-country skiing are allowed. Gasoline-powered motorboats are prohibited. Public programs are conducted daily in summer. A tiny nature center building is located at the main campground.

—R.L.

Kenneth Dubuque Memorial State Forest

Hawley/Plainfield/Savoy
7,822 acres

- **4.5 miles**
- **3.5 hours**
- **moderate**

Slightly off the beaten path is surely one way to describe Dubuque Memorial State Forest. Rugged, rocky, and remote are other fitting adjectives for this large, rather wild property. Huge ancient sugar maples stand guard over old stone fences and former farm fields. The forest lies a long way from any population center and is little visited today—but 175 years ago this ground and its bubbling waters supported a thriving agricultural community.

In the early nineteenth century the town of Hawley had a population of more than 1,000 residents. Farms, sawmills, a stone charcoal kiln (still standing), and a successful tannery provided employment. Charcoal kilns had huge appetites for wood, and this land looked very different than it does today. The farms were abandoned, though, and by 1970 only 224 people remained in Hawley. Some of the farmland was sold to the state early in this century, creating much of what we treasure as public conservation and recreation lands today. In 1980,

Kenneth Dubuque Memorial Forest

N

2100 feet

West Hawley Rd.

Hitchcock Meadow Trail

King Brook

stream

Hawley Pass Trail

P

Basin Brook

Basin Brook Trail

Moody Spring Trail

old beaver pond

King Corner Rd.

Hallockville Rd.

Hell's Kitchen Rd.

Basin Brook

Hawley State Forest was renamed to commemorate Kenneth Dubuque, a former forest supervisor who was instrumental in its establishment.

The land is reverting to northern hardwood forest, and in the process it is becoming a near-wilderness. Significant portions of the property lie above 1,600 feet elevation with red spruce, balsam fir, and small shrub swamps imparting a distinct boreal character to the landscape. The hilly, glacially scoured terrain is dissected by clear, cold, high-gradient streams. Lovely Basin Brook bounces over dark gray bedrock of folded schist covered with moss and lichens on its way to the Chickley River. Pure springs that once provided drinking water for the human inhabitants still percolate to the surface through glacial sands.

Patriarch trees of gargantuan proportions—spared long ago to provide shade or maple sugar—will catch your eye, but much of the forest is still quite young—new growth recolonizing land once cleared for pasturing or to make charcoal. That new growth now provides browse for white-tailed deer.

There are many miles of foot trails and former roads and other remnants of human occupation throughout Dubuque State Forest. The trails are in good condition although some are not well marked. None of the hills is particularly strenuous. From the parking area to the high point on the trail described below it is a vertical climb of 300 feet.

After parking in the dirt lot off West Hawley Road (elevation 1,350 feet), you might want to look at the painted forest map on the information kiosk situated on the left (a pit toilet is located directly behind it). Walk down the gated dirt King Corner Road—the settlement here is called King Corner—to start your hike. Cross wide King Brook and swing right, gradually ascending through woods of American beech (smooth, pale gray trunks), **enormous sugar maples,** very large yellow birches, and eastern hemlocks. Among the blooming flowers of midsummer you may see Indian tobacco, actually a lobelia with small light blue blossoms, and whorled wood aster. The delicate, light green fronds of New York fern are numerous and easy to identify (note that both ends of the frond are tapered). You'll also find the similar hay-scented fern, which grows well in rocky, partially sunny sites. The odor of its crushed foliage has never reminded me of the scent of hay, but you may feel differently.

After about 20 minutes of walking on the broad former roadway, come to Hawley Pass Trail, which crosses the road. Follow its blue and white painted blazes (some are faint) to the left. Unassuming greenish purple helleborine, an alien orchid, grows in the damp shaded soils here. The trail enters hemlock woods along an unnamed brook that you just crossed. Walk through beech/hemlock woods and eventually pass a big, split glacial erratic. If the day is moist, watch the path in front of you for bright orange red efts. Equipped with bright colors to warn potential predators of their poisonous skin secretions, red efts wander for up to seven years through woodlands prior to returning to the beaver pond environments where they hatched—to become aquatic redspotted newts.

The last portion of Hawley Pass Trail descends gradually to rocky Basin Brook, which it crosses, to an Adirondack shelter and picnic table (in disrepair) near its junction with Basin Brook Trail. Not far from the shelter grow **American yew shrubs;** female plants bear unique translucent fleshy red berries containing a single seed. Another name for this native shrub—ground hemlock—alludes to its resemblance to eastern hemlock. Yew needles, however, are longer and dark green on both sides. During an early August walk, we took a few moments to rest here by the brook. In the small sunlit clearing several beautiful white admiral butterflies flew about. We relaxed watching the boldly patterned black, white, blue, and red insects.

A short distance beyond the shelter the path crosses the brook and follows it upstream. About a mile away, Basin Brook enters the Chickley River, which flows northward to join the Deerfield. The Deerfield, of course, is a significant tributary of the Connecticut. Basin Brook almost seems to be more rock than water, as boulders and tilted bedrock layers—green with mosses and lichens—make up its channel in the small, narrow gorge. The setting is a lovely one and you'll enjoy your walk up along the gurgling stream. At a triangular blue marker,

Basin Brook gradually tumbles 350 vertical feet over moss-covered bedrock.

cross the brook again and continue to walk upstream along the opposite bank.

Soon you'll arrive at an old beaver pond surrounded by conifers. Old cuttings are still evident. (Beaver ponds gradually fill with silt, are abandoned by the rodents, and eventually become wet meadows.) The trail then veers away from Basin Brook, through cool spruce woods where sweet trilling dark-eyed juncos nest, to emerge from the forest onto Hallockville Road. The ground here is very sandy, a gift of the glaciers. Bracken fern grows along the sun-dappled roadsides. Predators like red fox often leave telltale signs of their nocturnal travels on paths and roadways. Tapered scats composed of fur, bones, and feathers are usually the only visual sign that a fox has passed by.

Turn left at Hallockville Road and walk a short distance to a small shrub swamp on the left. In late summer the attractive globular white flowers of buttonbush decorate the wetland. We were fortunate enough to hear the screams of a red-shouldered hawk and then to see this uncommon bird. Adult red-shouldereds are slightly smaller and slimmer than red-tails, have horizontally red-barred breasts, and banded black-and-white tails. Look also for the chestnut-colored shoulders of a perched bird. This declining species favors wetlands away from settlements and preys upon reptiles and amphibians in addition to rodents. Mosquitoes and deerflies are also present.

Retrace your steps back along Hallockville Road, passing the junction of Basin Brook Trail on the right. Follow old roadways from here back to the parking area—a distance of approximately two miles. On the left are deep sand deposits that show signs of former mining. Trembling aspen, white birch, northern red oak, and lowbush blueberries grow in the sterile soils. Unfortunately, off-road vehicle tires are aiding the wind in enlarging these "blowouts." Continue down (west) along the road a short distance to a small pond on your left at the junction of Hells Kitchen Road. Beautiful blue wild iris blooms in summer along the shore. Immediately beyond the pond, cross Basin Brook again.

Continue along the road, which borders beech/ maple forest, for about 10 minutes past the pond and turn right onto King Corner Road. Male olive green and white red-eyed vireos sing incessantly in the woodlands, proclaiming the boundaries of their nesting territories. Roger Tory Peterson has called this bird the most abundant bird of the eastern woodlands. The rich woodlands also contain perhaps our most beautiful and delicate fern—maidenhair. It's always a treat for me to find this attractive plant—which is not found in the acidic soils under evergreens. Climb gently now to the highest point along the route, reaching 1,660 feet above sea level about one-third of a mile past the turnoff from Hallockville Road.

After about 15 minutes of walking along the stone-wall-lined roadway, come to Hawley Pass Trail again— but continue straight on King Corner Road, crossing the unnamed brook and heading back up and then downhill to the parking area. In addition to specimen-size sugar maple, yellow birch, and hemlock trees, there are also some very big white ashes here—the tight-fitting bark of its long, straight trunk characteristically crosshatched. Ash seeds resemble canoe paddles, and the tough wood is used to manufacture ax handles and baseball bats among other things.

Getting There

From Route 116 in the center of Plainfield, take Route 116 west (and north) for 2.5 miles to its junction with Route 8A. Turn right onto Route 8A and travel north for 2.3 miles to a driveway on the right (opposite Stetson Road) leading to a dirt parking area adjacent to a State Forest maintenance shed.

Hours are sunrise to sunset. No fees. Horseback riding, cross-country skiing, and snowmobiling are permitted on some trails. A pit toilet is situated at the entrance.

—R.L.

Mohawk Trail State Forest
Charlemont/Savoy/Hawley
6,457 acres

Fall 96
winter 97/98 - twice

- **4 miles**
- **3 hours**
- **difficult**

Following the slow retreat of the mile-thick glacial ice sheet that gouged out much of the dramatic topography visible today, the swift-flowing Deerfield and Cold Rivers continued to cut through the uplands of western Franklin and eastern Berkshire Counties to produce spectacular narrow valleys and steep ridges. The Deerfield, a popular white-water stream, originates in the Green Mountains of southern Vermont and flows southward into Massachusetts, feeding the mighty Connecticut. The smaller Cold River has its source closer at hand—in the Hoosac Range of Berkshire County, just to the west. Their clear, cold waters intermingle at the northeastern edge of Mohawk Trail State Forest producing a land of spectacular beauty and numerous opportunities for varied outdoor adventures. White-water rafting and kayaking are very popular activities.

The forest trails wend steeply up the mountainsides but reward the hiker with sublime views of the Deerfield River valley. The steep slopes of Todd Mountain and nearby locations within the State Forest contain some of

Mohawk Trail State Forest

TO HOOSUC TUNNEL

River Rd.

Deerfield River

Clark Mountain

Indian Trail

Todd Mountain

Nature Trail

Cold River

Route 2

Thumper Mtn. Trail

Totem Trail

P

Forest Headquarters

N

1600 feet

the last vestiges of fabled old-growth forest remaining in the state. Black bear, bobcat, river otter, fisher, coyote, porcupine, and many smaller creatures inhabit this rugged terrain.

The region has a long and storied past. Route 2, today's principal east-west highway through northwestern Massachusetts, is known as the Mohawk Trail because it closely follows what was once the major trading route for peoples of the Iroquois nations between the Hudson and Connecticut Rivers. The path between the summits of Todd and Clark Mountains—still known as Indian Trail—is a surviving portion of the original trail used by Native Americans. Mohawk Trail State Forest was established in 1921.

After passing the contact station, park next to the headquarters buildings, immediately to the left near Cold River. In summer, nest boxes not far from the buildings often house beautiful blue-green and white tree swallows. Watch for adults arriving with crops full of insects for their ravenous young. On summer weekends, when the popular campground is usually full, walk along the paved road to the campground and trailhead. It takes about 15 minutes to reach the Indian Lookout Trail trailhead, on the right just before the road makes a sharp curve downhill to the left. Drinking water and rest rooms are available at the campground bathhouse.

Although it is only 1.25 miles from the trailhead to Todd Mountain Lookout, the trail is very steep for the first one-half hour or so until you reach the crest. Go slowly, take it easy, and enjoy the abundant plant and animal life along the way. At the lower elevations, russet-headed wood thrush and olive green red-eyed vireo provide musical accompaniment. Gorgeous **black-throated blue warbler** is one of the most common of its family in these woodlands. The male is deep blue and black above and clear white below, while his mate is drab brown but with a distinctive bright white wing patch. The abundant laurel and hobblebush thickets here provide them with ample nest sites. Listen for their distinctive, buzzy "beer-beer-beer-bee" songs.

On the dry, sunny, south-facing slopes of white and red oak and abundant witch hazel, trailing arbutus (mayflower)—the Massachusetts state flower—blooms in spring. Wintergreen produces white bell-shaped flowers in summer. Both are low growing. One of the tallest and most noticeable summer wildflowers of the gravelly slope is downy false foxglove, which sports large yellow, funnel-shaped blossoms. Interestingly, it is parasitic on oak roots.

After an elevation gain of almost 700 feet, reach the ridge crest, which connects the summits of Todd Mountain and Clark Mountain. Clark Mountain (1,920 feet) is heavily wooded and, although 200 feet higher than Todd, clear views are not possible from its top. This is the original **Indian Trail,** traversed by countless feet over the last three-plus centuries. Turn right to reach the summit of Todd Mountain. The crest trail passes through an abundance of mountain laurel, short red oaks, and lowbush blueberry, which ripen in August. Early azalea bushes are fairly numerous in the rocky soils between the two peaks; the gorgeous pink and very fragrant flowers appear in May.

Although the ridge trail won't take you through old-growth forest, the adjacent northern and eastern slopes of Todd Mountain are a sort of time capsule. **Four hundred-year-old eastern hemlock trees** stand high above the Deerfield River valley—a reminder of what this portion of western Massachusetts may have looked like before colonial settlement. These trees were spared

The view from the Indian Trail atop Todd Mountain is one of the most scenic in the region.

largely because harvesting these extremely steep slopes was deemed uneconomical. After less than one-half mile of very pleasant walking on the ridge crest, reach the rocky, partially open summit of Todd Mountain—more than 900 vertical feet above the trailhead.

I was thrilled to find rather fresh bear scat on the trail in the woods near the edge of the clearing. **Black bear,** the largest native mammal of our woodlands, is making an encouraging comeback as the state's forests mature. Consider yourself extremely fortunate if you happen upon one of these magnificent animals—something that's not likely to occur given their keen sense of smell and acute hearing. Black bears, despite their considerable size (adult males often weigh more than 300 pounds), are actually reluctant to make contact with humans—fleeing at the first sight, odor, or sound of you; the only exception being a mother bear and cub(s) that feel cornered and thus threatened.

Have a seat on the exposed bedrock and survey the splendid scene—from the southeast to the southwest the view is superb. Sitting in the sun on this lovely summit is an exhilarating experience, and you probably won't want to rush back down the mountain unless you have an urgent appointment to keep. **Indian Lookout**—from where Native Americans are said to have viewed the advance of colonial settlement up the valley—is situated a short distance farther; there the trail ends.

While returning along Indian Trail, listen and watch for the many species of birds that breed in these woodlands. I counted 33 species on an early July visit, of which 7 were colorful, active wood warblers. In an uncharacteristic moist tangle on the otherwise dry slope, I saw and heard two beautiful male Canada warblers as well as several fledglings. These birds usually inhabit wet, boggy sites. On my way back down the mountain I also encountered a very annoyed female ruffed grouse and her brood of fairly large chicks. Female grouse, in protecting their young, often make odd mewing sounds and sometimes even boldly charge the intruder—a behavior that startled me the first time I experienced it.

Be sure to turn left upon reaching the connecting trail to the campground rather than continuing straight on to Clark Mountain. Going steeply downhill can put a strain on the knees. After reaching the campground road, turn left and walk back to headquarters and your vehicle on the right.

For a slightly less strenuous walk with a nice view at the end, you might want to take Totem Trail to the 1,584-foot summit of an unnamed promontory due south of Todd Mountain. The trail begins on the opposite side of Route 2, just past a picnic area between the Cold River and Route 2, one mile west of the entrance road. Look for the Entering Pioneer Valley sign along Route 2 if you're arriving from the west. Park at a pullout just west of the picnic area on the north side of the road. A bronze plaque commemorating the establishment of the State Forest in 1921 is situated at this trailhead.

The round-trip distance for this trail through richer northern hardwood forest of birch, maple, beech, and hemlock is three miles. The rocks in the trail may be very slippery on a damp or humid day so watch your footing. Allow about one and one-half hours for this walk. Many ferns, especially spinulose wood fern, clubmosses, mosses, and fungi cover the floor of this damper, more shaded forest. The overlook, which is not as open as that on Todd Mountain, has views east into Trout Brook Cove and toward Hawks Mountain, the Deerfield River, and Route 2, which parallels it. During my July visit a red-tailed hawk soared over the ravine and two turkey vultures—quite close at hand—made several passes, riding the rising thermals of a midsummer morning.

Getting There

From the east: from the I-91 rotary in Greenfield, take Route 2 west for 19.0 miles to Charlemont. From the center of Charlemont, continue west on Route 2 for another 3.9 miles to the State Forest entrance road on the right. Cross the Cold River, and follow the road left to the contact station. Parking is just to the left—adjacent to headquarters. From the west: from the junction of Routes 8 and 2 in North Adams, take Route 2 east for 14.1 miles to the State Forest entrance on the left.

Hours are 9:30 A.M. to 8:00 P.M. for the picnic area. Access to the parking area near headquarters is always available. There is no parking fee for hikers; a $2 fee is collected for picnicking; camping fee is $6 per night; cabins may be rented for $16–$20 per night (minimum stays required, reservations strongly advised). Rest rooms and water are available at campground. Motorized vehicles are prohibited from trails; pets must be on a leash.

—R.L.

Hampshire and Hampden Counties

Buffam Falls Conservation Area
Pelham
65 acres

- **1 mile**
- **30 minutes**
- **easy**
- **great for children**

Buffam Falls Conservation Area is one of those lesser-known gems, far off the beaten path, worth the effort to find. Two small streams, Buffam Brook and Amethyst Brook, meet here in a woodland of tall hemlocks. The walk is short, relatively flat, and nice for children.

The entrance to the conservation area is about 400 feet north of the parking area on North Valley Road, just opposite the first house. A sign welcomes you to Buffam Falls Conservation Area and a small footbridge spans Buffam Brook. When you cross the footbridge, turn right. The path follows the brook downstream through shaded forest where mountain laurel grows in the understory beneath hemlocks and a scattering of pines.

It's only a 10-minute walk to the confluence of Buffam Brook and Amethyst Brook. The largest of the many **waterfalls** (all are relatively small) will be on your right, on Buffam Brook, just before the two brooks meet. Just beyond the falls, steps lead down to the confluence of the two brooks. This is a nice spot for photography, especially near noon when the sun is overhead and lights up the white cascading water and surrounding evergreens. The shaded waters stay cool even in the summer, and small brook trout hide beneath rocks near the riverbank.

In periods of low water it's possible to cross Amethyst Brook and follow another network of trails; however, this trail stays on this side (north) of the brook.

Retrace your path back up the steps and then take the trail with the white paint markers following Amethyst Brook upstream. (It will be on your right after climbing the steps.) The trail stays close to the stream, and as you pass through this dark ravine, the sound of flowing water mixes with birdcalls from the forest.

Much of this section of Pelham and the western portion of Amherst have been left in their natural state to protect this important watershed, and the diversity of wildlife is rich. Deer, wild turkey, raccoon, and otter are just some of the animals seen on the property. Although once abundant when Europeans first settled in New England, **turkeys** were wiped out in Massachusetts by 1851 from overhunting and destruction of the birds' hardwood habitat. Through a program of trapping wild turkeys in New York and transplanting them in Massachusetts, beginning in 1972, their numbers are now increasing throughout the Bay State.

In spite of their increasing numbers, they are difficult to see in the woods. Generally, they see you before you see them, and their coloring blends in well with the woods. One time I came upon a flock of wild turkeys and was amazed at how fast they could move, silently weaving through the undergrowth. They look similar to the barnyard turkey but have a rusty (not white) tip to the tail and are a bit slimmer.

Turkeys feed on acorns, wild turnip, jack-in-the-pulpit, and early buds of hardwoods. In the springtime the male "toms" try to attract females by strutting with tail fan erect. Toms weigh an average of 16 pounds and females about 9 or 10 pounds. And unlike the domestic-bred turkeys, which are too heavy to fly, these wild birds can take to the wing at 35 miles per hour!

Hemlocks shade the cool waters at Buffam Falls.

As you walk along Amethyst Brook, the **hemlock** needles that cushion your steps also serve to keep the undergrowth down, thus allowing you to scan the woods for wildlife. Hemlock trees block out much of the sun, and their acidic needles also help to keep vegetation from growing beneath their sweeping branches.

After you've walked about 10 minutes down this streamside trail, it climbs to the left a bit, rising away from the stream, and connects with another trail. By turning left the trail forms a loop, leading back toward Buffam Brook.

More-ambitious hikers may want to turn right and explore the trail to the east, which leads through a pine grove. The trail roughly follows Amethyst Brook upstream for about half a mile and then crosses Meetinghouse Road. Leave the trail and turn left (north) and go along the dirt road for 0.4 mile to an old barn on the left. To the left is a path; follow it westerly. This will lead you downstream along Buffam Brook and back to the entrance at the footbridge.

(There are additional interesting trails to explore nearby at the Amethyst Brook Conservation Area. The parking lot for this area is found on Pelham Road, roughly one mile west from where it passes North Valley Road.)

Getting There

From the junction of Route 202 and Amherst Road (at the Pelham Town Hall) take Amherst Road west about 2.0 miles to the United Church of Pelham (where Meetinghouse Road and Enfield Road intersect with Amherst Road). From this intersection continue west on Amherst Road exactly 1.2 miles to North Valley Road on the right. Turn right on North Valley Road and go 0.6 mile to the pull-off on the left under the power lines.

From Amherst take Main Street east to where it crosses North East Street and continue 1.7 miles (Main Street turns into Pelham Road). Turn left on North Valley Road and go 0.6 mile to the pull-off on the left under the power lines.

Open year-round, seven days a week, no admission, no rest rooms.

—M.T.

William Cullen Bryant Homestead

Cummington

195 acres

- •0.9 mile
- •1 hour
- •easy

This little rill, that from the springs
Of yonder grove its current brings,
Plays on the slope awhile, and then
Goes prattling into groves again,
Oft to its warbling waters drew
My little feet, when life was new.

So begins William Cullen Bryant's "The Rivulet," written in 1823 at his home, now a property of The Trustees of Reservations. This poem is one of many written by the poet and newspaperman during his long and productive life. In 1799, as a child of five, Bryant moved to the big two-and-one-half-story home on the hill, now a National Natural Landmark, where he spent the happiest days of his youth. Years later, after gaining fame and fortune as poet and editor of the *Saturday Evening Post*, he returned to his boyhood home amid the rolling, wooded hills of rural Hampshire County. He lived out his later years tending orchards—he and his brother planted

William Cullen Bryant Homestead

West Cummington Road

N

500 feet

barn

P

pasture

homesite

Rivulet Brook

Route 112

Bryant Road

Route 112

1,300 fruit trees and rows of now massive sugar maples paralleling the stone walls—and walking the woods and fields until his death in 1878 at age 84.

From the small gravel parking lot (elevation 1,560 feet) across from the homestead, walk back down the road 300 feet. Walk through a gap in the stone wall to the left and cross the pasture to West Cummington Road. In late summer insects abound in the grass. Field crickets chirp endlessly on warm days as butterflies seek nectar and mates. Watch for fritillaries, monarchs, red-spotted purple-white admirals, viceroys, large wood nymphs, inornate ringlets, sulphurs, and whites. Rivulet Trail begins on the opposite side of the road. When crossing the pasture is not advisable due to the presence of dairy cows, walk to the intersection of Route 112 (Bryant Four Corners), turn left, and walk north on West Cummington Road for approximately 300 feet to the trailhead on the right. Yellow circular paint blazes mark the trail route.

The forest floor is cushioned with decaying pine needles, providing the perfect seed bed for **Canada mayflower** and other acid-tolerant wildflowers. Rivulet Brook, which is spring fed, flows year-round, tumbling along, twisting and turning. In summer listen for the songs of wood warblers and scan the tree branches for

An inherent tranquillity overhangs the pasture and woodland as seen from the homestead.

American redstart, Canada warbler, rose-breasted grosbeak, red-eyed vireo, and tiny red-breasted nuthatch. Besides sugar maple and white pine, white ash and black cherry are fairly numerous and some are quite large. As the trail descends gradually through a small hemlock gorge, see that many of the hemlocks are sizable, creating thick shade below. The bark of very old hemlocks tends to become a reddish cinnamon color. Where the stream has cut deeply—leaving high banks—the exposed roots of hemlocks are clearly visible. In the stream itself, flat moss-covered stones harbor dusky salamanders. Spinulose wood fern (an evergreen), shining clubmoss—which looks something like a green bottle brush—and numerous fungi protrude from the moist soil. Red squirrels eat the abundant toadstools.

I counted the growth rings of one hemlock that had been cleared from the trail and found 85—a mere youngster amid these towering giants. Where more sunlight is available, **yellow birch,** one of the northern hardwood forest codominants, has grown to truly unusual size. Nowhere else in western Massachusetts have I seen such large specimens. In spring the woodland floor brightens with the three-petaled blossoms of painted and red trilliums and violets (which Bryant mentions in his poem). Christmas fern, long beech fern (whose bottom leaflets point downward), and New York fern grow in the rich soils below the big trees. The songs of wood thrushes resound through the woodland at dusk and at dawn.

Progress down along the north side of the brook. The ravine becomes progressively deeper. Clay banks have been eroded and exposed by powerful floodwaters. Rivulet Brook flows into the Westfield River just 0.7 mile north of the trailhead.

At the lowest point on the route (1,390 feet) cross a wooden bridge. The trail turns left to begin the return just before reaching two very large white pines just off the trail—look for double yellow blazes. These trees are so large, I photographed them with a friend standing alongside for scale. Although not shown on the official Trustees map of the property, the trail now makes a loop at its terminus and rejoins the main trail near the brook. Red-backed salamanders and red efts patrol the moist woodlands looking for insects and other small invertebrates to eat. Red efts are bold enough to be abroad in daylight, especially if it's raining; they are poisonous to predators. Beechnuts litter the trail below the smooth, light-gray-skinned trees in late summer. Wild turkeys, bear, squirrels, and other wildlife are fond of the nutritious nuts.

Work your way slowly uphill and back to the trailhead, and think about how these woods may have changed since Bryant's youth. Some of the trees are much older and much larger to be sure. The landscape, rather than predominantly farmland as it was in his day, is now largely wooded. In many ways, however, little has probably changed in this rural setting—something that would no doubt please the poet were he alive today.

Getting There

From the east: take Route 9 west to Cummington and turn left onto Route 112. Follow Route 112 for 1.5 miles to the Bryant Four Corners. Continue straight on the maple and stone-wall-lined road that leads to the homestead on your left and the small parking area opposite, which can accommodate about six vehicles. From the west: turn right onto Route 112 in West Cummington just before it crosses the Westfield. Follow Route 112 west and south to the Bryant Four Corners and turn right to enter the property.

Reservation closes at sunset. No admission fee. House hours are Friday, Saturday, and Sunday, 1:00–5:00 P.M. Admission fee to house. Rest rooms located inside. Picnic tables available across from parking area.

—R.L.

Chesterfield Gorge
Chesterfield
161 acres

7/5/97

- **3 miles**
- **2 hours**
- **easy**

You will find no other place in Massachusetts quite like this one. Chesterfield Gorge has that kind of primeval beauty embodied by solid rock and flowing water. The corrosive power of water and glacial ice are clearly evident in the sheer gray granite chasm; gouged and sculpted bedrock bears the legacy of grinding glaciers, followed by millennia of polishing by water. The margins of this lovely fast-flowing stream—designated a National Wild and Scenic River in 1994—are lined with smooth oval granite cobbles. The shallow rocky bottom makes this ideal habitat for cold-water fishes such as brook, brown, and rainbow trout.

Stately white pines and hemlocks line the east side of the narrow gorge. Oaks, birches, and beeches thrive in the sun on the opposite side. Interrupted fern, sedges, horsetails, and willows grow in the moist floodplain slightly downstream of the chasm.

At the upper end of the gorge—"the narrows"— stand the stone abutments of the **historic High Bridge.** Built in 1739, the bridge enabled the Boston-to-Albany

Chesterfield Gorge

River Road

P

cellar holes

Whitside Brook

The Gorge

▲
926'

↑
N

300 feet

Westfield River

↔ River Road

Post Road to span the Westfield. British troops crossed the bridge retreating to Boston following their defeat at Saratoga in 1777. A tollgate was erected on the opposite (east) side of the river in 1779, and the remnants of the gatekeeper's house and the surrounding small community are all that remain. This Trustees of Reservations property was acquired in 1929 in a successful attempt to prevent it from being logged. Additional parcels were added later, and the reservation is bordered by the 2,000-acre Gilbert Bliss State Forest.

This is a rather flat, easy walk. From the parking area, a short trail skirts the top of the bluff above the river, affording wonderful sights and sounds of the gorge and river. Continue to walk downstream and slightly downhill where the path rejoins River Road to the right. Beyond the gorge you can access the rich natural community along the river from many short informal trails leading from the road.

After parking and reading the notices on the visitor information board—where a map is posted—proceed directly to the gorge overlook area. Be aware that **poison ivy** grows abundantly in the reservation. Walk down through the grassy, well-kept picnic area, on the right, to the trail leading to the edge of the defile. Metal railings provide a measure of safety. From here, gaze southward (right) and downstream through the narrows. The view is truly inspirational and you may want to capture it on film. (Relatively high film speeds are recommended.) The **sheer granite walls** are topped by a thick growth of eastern hemlock. The ground beneath your feet is spongy with the accumulated layers of decayed and decaying needles. Little else can grow in this acidic soil, so rich in tannin.

After you've enjoyed the views, continue to where the trail intersects River Road and turn left onto the road. Follow the gurgling river downstream. Across the river are forests of beech, birch, and maple. Mountain laurel

The 100-foot-deep chasm bears witness that even granite is no match for the gouging action of flowing water over the eons.

(which blooms beautifully in late June and early July) provides an evergreen shrub layer. Hobblebush, another understory shrub, produces large clusters of white hydrangea-like flowers in May. Ferns and little club-mosses grow on the forest floor. Spring's wildflower extravaganza yields such finds as Solomon's seal (with white flowers hanging in pairs along the stem); false Solomon's seal; Canada mayflower (all three are lilies); wild sarsaparilla, which has round heads of modest yellow flowers on long stalks; red trillium, or wake-robin; and white starflower.

About 700 feet beyond the end of the reservation trail on the right you'll pass Whitside Brook, a modest but lovely cascading stream that flows over moss-covered boulders on its way to the Westfield. The steep slopes beyond the brook are clothed by hemlock and pine. Impish red squirrels bound across the forest floor or chatter at an intruder from above. You may also see smaller striped eastern chipmunks.

The river makes a swing to the east. Beyond the gorge, the floodplain widens. Explore the rocky riverbanks in late spring and early summer. Among the colorful wildflowers blooming in the sunny but moist river corridor are pink wild geranium, golden alexanders, robin plantain (actually a daisy relative), tall buttercup, and pretty marsh blue violet. When you look back upstream to the north you'll see the rounded green mass of Smith Pyramid—500 feet above the river. At 1,185 feet, it is the highest point in the area.

During a visit in early June, I was fortunate to see a female **common merganser** and her seven ducklings. This large fish-eating duck is a rare breeder in Massachusetts. The female, with her soft gray body plumage and slightly crested, rust-colored head, made loud barking sounds while half swimming, half running over the surface of the water, urging her young to follow her, which they did. In seconds, they were out of sight. Common mergansers have serrated bills well designed for gripping slippery fish. Here they feed on common shiners and other small fishes. However, you're more likely to find the blue-and-white, shaggy-crested belted kingfisher hunting here. The female is the more colorful of the pair, with a chestnut "belt" across her abdomen as well as a blue one.

Continue down the dirt road, passing a huge fern- and moss-covered boulder on the right. Listen for the songs of such forest-dwelling birds as eastern wood pewee, veery, wood thrush, and rose-breasted grosbeak. Mosquitoes are numerous in late spring and summer so you may want to bring repellent. Far more welcome are beautiful butterflies that bask, feed, and puddle in woodland clearings and along the riverbanks. Big yellow and black tiger swallow-tails were in the process of emerging from their pupal cases during one of my late spring visits. The sight of a dozen of these gorgeous insects probing for mineral salts on a gravel bank was a memorable one indeed.

If you look carefully into the shallows you'll see inch-long caddis fly larval cases constructed of sticks by these insects. Watch closely and you may see the animals crawling slowly about, dragging their homes with them. Larger aquatic invertebrates in the river include three-and-one-half-inch-long crayfish. Emerging mayflies provide food for trout. Fishing here is by artificial lure only and strictly catch and release. The state Division of Fisheries and Wildlife has posted many fishing access sites along the river, and trout fishing is, as you might expect, a popular pastime.

Proceed another few hundred yards (1.45 miles from the parking area) to a closed iron gate at the State Forest boundary. A small feeder stream flows under the road near this point. Bronze-colored **two-lined salamanders** spend their days under flat stones along the wet margin of the brook.

Retrace your steps back to your vehicle (about 1.5 miles) to explore the historic, human-made features of this property, or continue walking along River Road to the Knightville Reservoir in Huntington—a distance of 6.0 miles.

After returning to your vehicle at the lot (parking is not allowed along River Road), continue north approximately 200 feet beyond the parking area on informal trails to a vantage point on the west side of the river, opposite the High Bridge abutment. You can get a nice view of the native stone structure from this spot. Continuing to the left down to river level, see examples of **sculpted bedrock,** left of the abutment. The Westfield makes another 90-degree turn here to the east. When you're ready, head back toward the parking lot, and cross the road to view cellar holes remaining from the early settlement. In early May, a thick stand of lovely bloodroot carpets the edge of the clearing with delicate white blossoms.

Getting There

From Route 143 in Chesterfield, travel 2.0 miles to West Chesterfield, cross the Westfield River, and almost immediately turn left onto Ireland Street (no sign) opposite Cummington Road. Travel 0.8 mile down Ireland Street to gravel River Road on the left. You'll see the green-and-white Trustees of Reservations sign for the gorge here. Drive down River Road for 0.2 mile to the parking area on your left.

Hours are sunrise to sunset. Entry fee is $1.50 for adults; children under age twelve are free. Pit toilets are available. Dogs allowed on leash only. Swimming, bathing, and wading are prohibited.

—R.L.

Glendale Falls Reservation
Middlefield
60 acres

- **1.2 miles**
- **1.5 hours**
- **moderate**

Clear and cold, Glendale Brook flows headlong over polished **granite ledges** forming gleaming white cascades and root-beer-colored pools as it rushes toward the Middle Branch of the Westfield River. Pleasantly out of the way, Glendale Falls is actually a series of picturesque cascades, more than 150 feet high in all (making it the highest in Massachusetts). The volume pouring over the rust-stained ledges is quite considerable—especially in spring—and a visit is well worth your while at any time.

From the top of the falls (1,060 feet) is a beautiful view eastward of the wooded ridges on the far side of the Middle Branch—some reaching 1,600 feet above sea level. All three branches of the Westfield were declared a National Wild and Scenic River in 1994. Eastern hemlocks grow on the north-facing slope right of the falls, while birch, beech, and maple stand on the sunnier opposing side. Mountain laurel and hobblebush grow beneath the dominant trees. The only way to view the falls themselves is to walk down the rather steep, rocky hill to a point below the cascades, stopping quite often to take in the photogenic scenes above.

Glendale Falls Reservation

old foundations

Glendale Falls

East River Road

Middle Branch

Clark Wright Road

Old Logging Road

Glendale Brook

N

1/8 mile

P

Native stone foundations of two buildings, one possibly a former mill house, stand on the northern shore, and a big **granite mill wheel**—looking like a huge doughnut—lies abandoned along the edge of the cascades. Upstream of the falls are wetlands and upland meadows that in the 1700s were part of the Glendale

An abandoned granite millstone rests in the pools along Glendale Brook.

Farm. Now The Trustees of Reservations owns and manages this lovely property.

There is no formal trail to the base of the falls, but it is possible from the parking area to cross the brook above the falls easily on stepping-stones adjacent to the parking lot. Proceed downhill through the deciduous forest on the north side of the cascades. **Witch hazel,** a small tree from which the astringent of the same name is derived, is quite abundant. Unlike most plants, this tree blooms in late fall, producing somewhat straggly yellow blossoms. Its leaves are wavy toothed and have uneven bases. Other understory trees you'll see include the aptly named ironwood (also known as musclewood); striped maple, or moosewood (green-and-white-striped bark); the scaly barked hop hornbeam; and the white-flowering Juneberry, or shad. The name shad refers to the fact that gizzard shad (a herring relative) made their spring migrations up streams from salt water at the time that this tree flowered.

From vantage points along the way, you'll be able to get intimate looks at the gushing water and the dark, tannin-stained pools between the numerous cascades. Small pools host tiny shiners, and numerous water striders skate across the water's elastic surface film. Miniature sand beaches lie where floodwaters deposited their loads, and here moisture-loving plants like gray willow and spotted touch-me-not have gained a foothold. Delicate in appearance, clematis, or virgin's bower, vines snake out over rocks while sedges grow grasslike in the crevices between them. An uncommon species of fern, **fragile fern,** also thrives in the moist crevices between the moss-covered boulders. Long beech fern is a small species that can be identified by the fact that its lowest leaflets point decidedly downward. Look for it as well as Christmas and marginal wood ferns in the rich woodland, while seeking interrupted and sensitive ferns in wet spots.

In spring, when the cascades roar with their greatest volume, the forest floor brightens briefly with the white blossoms of Canada mayflower and false Solomon's seal, yellow sessile-leaved bellwort (also known as wild oats), greenish yellow clintonia, red trillium, and white starflower. In summer look for tall meadow rue as it extends its starry white flowers; tall buttercup, which is in bloom; robin plantain, really a composite with purplish and yellow daisylike flowers; and wild roses that show off their delicate pink blossoms.

Listening for birdsong over the tumult of flowing water isn't easy. But you may hear the songs of solitary and red-eyed vireos, ovenbird, black-throated green and Blackburnian warblers (arguably our most beautiful, found usually in the hemlocks), and the long, loud, bubbling song of our smallest wren—**winter wren.** Hemlock gorges dissected by brooks are the favorite haunts of this bird.

You can walk about a half mile downstream before returning to work your way back up the rather steep slope. Hiking up will take you about 15 to 20 minutes. Deer come to the stream to drink and browse on the succulent vegetation, but you'll probably find only their tracks unless you happen to be here at dawn or dusk. Raccoons, too, find food along the brook, hunting with their sensitive noses and dexterous paws.

For a very different walk, cross Clark Wright Road and stroll along the old logging road (no markings, but fairly easy to follow) that roughly follows rocky Glendale Brook upstream. The brook's main sources actually number six. The wet meadow clearings are good places to search for keen-eyed dragonflies, butterflies, and other insects. On a June visit, I was happy to find an attractive arctic skipper, a small, uncommon orangish butterfly that lives in wet boreal environments. Other summer butterflies you may well see include tiger swallowtail, red-spotted purple/white admiral (now considered the same species by lepidopterists), spring azure, and little wood satyr. Birds that prefer brushy thickets dwell here and include gray catbird, a mockingbird relative. This bird's catlike meow is unmistakable. In wetter habitats look for beautiful nesting yellow, black, and blue Canada warblers, and listen for the sweet trill of rusty-capped swamp sparrows emanating from the marshy growth. You can walk for about one-half mile before the track becomes overgrown, then retrace your steps to your car in the reservation parking lot.

Getting There

From Route 143 in West Chesterfield where you'll cross the Westfield River, travel west for 2.25 miles to the junction with Route 112. Stay left and travel just under 2.0 miles to the intersection of Routes 143/112 at Worthington Corners. Turn right and travel north on Route 143 for approximately 2.2 miles to where it bears left. After driving west and then south for just over 1.5 miles, you'll come to River Road. Turn left and follow River Road south. After 3.25 miles, you'll come to Cone Hill (Smith Hollow) Road on the right, but stay left on River Road. You'll be paralleling the Middle Branch. After traveling just over 5.3 miles since your original turn onto River Road, turn right onto Clark Wright Road and travel uphill for 0.4 mile to the Glendale Falls Reservation gravel parking area on the right—just before you would cross the brook.

Reservation hours are sunrise to sunset. There are no fees, picnic areas, or rest rooms. Camping, fires, motorized vehicles, and firearms are prohibited. There is no map currently available from the Trustees for this property.

—R.L.

Arcadia Wildlife Sanctuary
Easthampton/Northampton
550 acres

- **1.75 miles**
- **1 hour**
- **easy**
- **great for children**

Situated in the floodplain of the Connecticut River valley, Arcadia Wildlife Sanctuary is a great birding location with five miles of trails, traversing forest, and marsh. This Massachusetts Audubon Society sanctuary borders the Mill River and an ancient oxbow of the Connecticut River where migrating birds stop to rest. An observation tower, overlooking a marsh, provides great views and is a big hit with children!

To begin, take the trail to the Old Coach Road to the right of the nature center, into woods of maple, oak, hemlock, and white pine. Be sure to pause for a moment near the rear of the building and scan the bird feeder and nearby trees. On my last visit, a number of goldfinches were flashing brilliantly in the sunshine as they flew from the trees to the feeder.

There is also a **vernal pool** just beyond the bird feeder. These freshwater pools usually dry up by midsummer, but during the spring they are alive with amphibians: listen for the "peep" of the spring peepers or the

Arcadia Wildlife Sanctuary

"quack" of a wood frog. Because vernal pools are temporary, no fish live in them, which means that the eggs laid by frogs and salamanders will not be eaten. Vernal pools are also rich in nutrients for tadpoles and salamander larvae to feed upon. The drying of the pools in the summer helps speed the decomposition rate of organic matter, which in turn supplies nutrients. (Amphibians face increasing peril as development destroys vernal pools and pesticides work their way into the food chain. There is also concern that depletion of the ozone layer and corresponding increase in ultraviolet radiation is harming amphibian eggs.)

Our walk continues past the vernal pool and swampy area on the Old Coach Road Trail. This trail leads in a northwesterly direction along a ridge that parallels the Mill River a few hundred feet to your right. Pass over an abandoned trolley line that connected Northampton to Springfield in the nineteenth century. Mountain laurel emerges in the understory, making this particular path a great place to walk in the spring. A number of trails intersect the Old Coach Trail, but you should continue on this trail, traveling straight until you reach Hitchcock Brook.

The trail descends a hill at Hitchcock Brook. Bear right rather than cross the brook. In a hundred feet, you reach the River Trail at a backwater of the Mill River called Wood Duck Pond, which, as the name implies, is good habitat for the brilliantly colored **wood duck.** Males have patterns of purple, green, yellow, red, and blue. The female is less colorful but can be identified by its white eye ring. Look for them soaking up the sun on a dead tree branch above the water or feeding on the pond. They are tremendous fliers, capable of dodging trees at great speed.

The nesting boxes you see at the pond are constructed to duplicate the hollow trees wood ducks prefer, using an entrance hole small enough to keep out raccoons. Females line the nest boxes with down plucked from their breasts and incubate the eggs with body heat. When the ducklings hatch, they respond to their mothers' calls and jump from the nests, following the mothers to the safety of the water.

Follow the River Trail to the east where it becomes Fern Trail. Footprints in the mud along the banks of the Mill River may reveal the tracks of raccoon, mink, and the large hand-size prints of great blue heron. If great blue heron find a hunting site to their liking, they will often visit the same place day after day to catch fish. I once saw a heron in the exact same spot for more than 30 days!

The trail passes by a diversity of ferns, including ostrich ferns with three- to five-foot fronds, and towering shagbark hickory as it follows the Mill River to an **observation tower.** Rising roughly 60 feet, the tower is a great place to rest and scan Arcadia Marsh. Below the tower on a post, two signs mark the high-water level of the floods of 1936 and 1984.

From the observation tower, continue following Fern Trail to an old orchard. On my trip I had the good fortune to see a pileated woodpecker here: a large, rather uncommon woodpecker, roughly the size of a crow with

Arcadia's observation tower overlooks marsh and forest.

an identifying red crest. You might also see a cardinal. During spring, listen for the bird's series of loud, clear whistles it uses to announce its territory prior to mating. Also be on the lookout for bluebirds, bobolinks, and red-winged blackbirds that frequent the orchard.

Bear to the left at the orchard onto Cedar Trail and continue to follow the Mill River downstream. A five-minute walk will bring you to the mouth of Mill River where it meets the **Connecticut River Oxbow,** subject of a wonderful painting by Thomas Cole. Prior to 1841, the Connecticut River flowed through this loop. During high water, however, the river abandoned a bend to create a more direct downstream course, leaving the oxbow as a lake.

To return to the parking lot, simply retrace your steps back to the orchard and follow the Horseshoe Trail a short distance southwestward to the nature center. The orchard you pass through has old apple trees and cherry trees, a favorite source of food for cedar waxwings and other birds.

Getting There

From I-91, take the Northampton exit (Exit 18). From the exit ramp, turn right onto Route 5 south. Follow this for almost 1.5 miles and make a right turn onto East Street at a road sign for Easthampton center. Follow East Street for a little more than 1.0 mile and turn right onto Fort Hill Road (marked by a Massachusetts Audubon Society sign). Travel 1.0 mile to the sanctuary entrance.

Open year-round, closed Mondays except for major holidays, admission fee (MAS members free), rest rooms, nature center.

—M.T.

Joseph Allen Skinner
State Park
Hadley/South Hadley
390 acres   *Fall 96*

- **1.75 miles**
- **2.5 hours**
- **difficult**

For years, I drove from my home in the Berkshires to Northampton and points east along Route 66, enjoying a wonderful view of the Holyoke Range and its gleaming white summit building. I often wondered what the building was and about the view possible from it. One early September day, I finally made up my mind to find out.

Mt. Holyoke, the nominal western end of the **basaltic Mt. Holyoke Range,** rises more than 800 feet above the broad meanders of the Connecticut River. Some 200 million years ago, two lava flows spilled forth through a crack in the earth's crust, solidifying to form the Holyoke Range. This rock, rich in iron, has oxidized to a dark reddish hue. It fractures along hexagonal planes and produces a distinctive metallic "clink" when struck against another piece of basalt.

The mountain's summit is the site of America's oldest mountain resort, a one-room building constructed in 1821. Later additions and renovations gave rise to the current Summit House. Once it had 70 rooms and

Joseph Allen Skinner State Park

Connecticut River

Hockanum Rd.

conglomerated
rock

MAIN
ENTRANCE

Halfway
House

Summit
House

Mtn. Rd.

P

M-M Trail

Route 47

N

1000 feet

catered to the nation's wealthy and famous. The hurricane of 1938 destroyed most of it. Between 1854 and 1942 a funicular (cable) railway transported millions of tourists to the summit. J. A. Skinner donated the property to the commonwealth in 1938, and it officially opened as a state facility in 1940.

Today you can drive to the top but it is far more enjoyable to walk. From the largely open summit, assuming the day is clear, you can gaze out upon the flat, fertile fields of the Connecticut River valley, some of the richest farmland in mostly rocky New England. Millions of years of erosion and sedimentation together with thousands of years of spring floods have deposited a thick layer of rich silt in this broad floodplain. Beyond the valley, you can make out all the major promontories within about a 60-mile radius, including Mt. Snow in Vermont, New Hampshire's Mt. Monadnock (where the 117-mile-long Metacomet-Monadnock [M-M] Trail terminates), and Mt. Greylock in the Berkshires.

Park in the designated area (with room for 8 to 10 vehicles) located left off Mountain Road, just before the road makes a sharp swing to the left to begin the ascent to the top. The road is sometimes gated at this point. The Two Forest Trail begins at the rear of the parking area and proceeds left. It is marked with yellow paint blazes. The starting elevation is about 325 feet above sea level.

Walk over level ground through deciduous forest for a short distance and then climb briefly and steeply to the next plateau along the road. The leaves dropped each fall by the big black birches, gray birches, sugar and red maples, and other trees help to produce a fertile bed for tiny clubmosses, ferns (especially evergreen wood fern and hay-scented fern), and spring wildflowers—false Solomon's seal (which has its flowers at the tip whereas the flowers of Solomon's seal are at the nodes), Solomon's seal, Canada mayflower (also known as wild lily of the valley), and partridgeberry. In late summer, white snakeroot and white aster are abundant. Thousands of ankle-high red oak seedlings will indicate that a bountiful crop of acorns was produced the previous season. Hemlocks become prominent on the slopes, especially to your left. Black-capped chickadees (the Massachusetts state bird) dangle acrobatically from the branches and bigger, noisy crested blue jays fill the air with their piercing calls. The trail proceeds east-northeast, and if you peer through the hemlocks you'll see cornfields in the valley to the north. Flocks of Canada geese, with their ever vigilant sentinels keeping a watchful eye; American crows; wild turkeys; and other wildlife eagerly glean the waste grain after fall harvest.

Continue straight on Two Forest Trail. Soon your eyes fall upon a huge cabin-sized basalt boulder known as the **Devil's Football,** because of its odd shape. How did it come to rest here? The rough, hexagonally fissured surface and color add considerably to the comparison. Unfortunately, human graffiti mar its surface. Several trails merge at this point. Follow the Devil's Football Trail (blazed blue and yellow) straight to Mountain Road and the Halfway House. A short trail also goes sharply right up to Mountain Road. You should continue straight. At 0.75 mile cross the paved road just below the Halfway House—park headquarters—which you may wish to visit upon your return. You'll be able to see a big gear wheel once part of the old railway system to the summit.

After crossing Mountain Road and walking a short distance to the left, pick up the trail, which becomes noticeably steeper, utilizing a switchback to the left to ascend the dark hemlock slope. Retaining walls have been built to help counteract the force of gravity. The trail is in good condition but stopping often to catch your breath may be a necessity, as it was for me. From here, it's 0.75 mile to the top. Eastern chipmunks are the most visible mammals in late summer. While you rest you can't help but notice these attractively striped ground squirrels running about, often with cheek pouches crammed full of acorns for the winter larder. They emit shrill chirps and birdlike clucks.

Near the summit the trail forks—stay to the left. When the trail splits again, take the right fork and walk up to the **Summit House** at an elevation of 940 feet. From here parts of four states are visible on a clear day, and interpretive panels on the deck of the building identify major features of the landscape. Other panels relate the interesting history of the Summit House. Gravel walks lead through a manicured picnic area with wonderful views of the Connecticut Valley where you may want to stop for a snack.

Following a brief but energetic rain shower that September morning, I noticed a wispy cloud of what turned out to be one-quarter-inch-long winged ants just above the picnic area. The smokelike column of insects was made up of many thousands of ants that, having left the hive, represented an expeditionary force seeking to colonize new ground. The ants were mating and the young queens moved off to found new colonies. During the dramatic clearing following the storm, the bushes and trees attracted my attention as fall migrant songbirds flitted about in search of sustenance. In a few minutes I was able to spot black-throated green warblers, an American redstart, a magnolia warbler, and three red-eyed vireos.

When you're ready to move on, retrace your steps, but take the left (westerly) fork below the Summit House this time. Follow the blue-and-white-blazed M-M Trail. Rock walls indicate that this ridge once pastured livestock. Enter an oak/hickory woodland of rather low stature. The forest floor is sun flecked, and basaltic outcrops up to 10 feet high punctuate the open ridge-top woodlands. Little bluestem grass, which fades to a rose wine color in late summer, grows in clumps among the rocks. Mountain ash, sporting clusters of bright red berries, and chinquapin oak, a generally southern species, do well on the thin soils of the Holyoke Range. In spring and fall keep one eye on the sky as hawks set sail on the warm updrafts created by the ridge. Broad-winged (about the size of a crow, with a fan-shaped black-and-white-banded tail), small, long-tailed sharp-shinned, and big resident red-tailed hawks all ride the rising thermals.

Follow the white-blazed M-M Trail as it descends rather steeply for a brief period then skirts the escarpment edge, affording you a nice view of the valley to the northwest. Descend slightly again and cross a basalt outcrop of the ridge where the **columnar cleavage** of the former lava is readily evident. In places, freezing and thawing have created convenient natural staircases, and the rough texture of this rock makes for sure footing even on flat, glacier-scoured sections. Northern red oak, pignut hickory, fuzzy-stemmed staghorn sumac, wild rose, and raspberry represent the predominant woody growth of the ridge here. After about 25 minutes of walking from

Mountain ash, with its rich red berries, dots the landscape at J. A. Skinner State Park.

the Summit House, come to an open spot where the hill drops away gradually and a truly wonderful view of the largest Massachusetts city in the valley—Springfield—is visible to the south as is the Connecticut River.

While scanning the horizon with my binoculars, I chanced upon a huge dark bird soaring northwesterly near the river. The brilliant white head and tail told me without a doubt that I was admiring an adult bald eagle! Perhaps this individual was one of the birds now nesting at the Quabbin Reservoir 15 miles east of here (see p. 87). A very successful hacking program has returned nesting bald eagles to Massachusetts. Young birds from Canada were brought to the Quabbin in the 1980s in hopes that they would eventually come to see the place as home and choose to nest there when mature at age five.

The overlook is a convenient spot to turn around and retrace your steps back to below the Summit House to follow the Halfway House Trail (blue blazes), left, back the way you came—eventually to your car along Mountain Road. A reasonably fast walk will get you back to your vehicle in less than one hour if you're in a hurry.

Getting There

From the junction of Routes 116 and 47 in South Hadley take Route 47 north for 3.5 miles to Mountain Road (Barrus Road on some maps) on the right. Follow Mountain Road for 0.4 mile to the small roadside parking area on the left just before Mountain Road turns sharply left.

Alternately, from the Route 9 exit ramp off the I-91 ramp in Northampton, follow Route 9 east across the Connecticut River on the Calvin Coolidge Bridge. Follow Route 9 for 1.9 miles to Route 47 (Middle Street) on the right. Route 47 makes a 90-degree turn to the left (east) after 0.6 mile. Continue on Route 47 for 3.8 more miles to Mountain Road on the left. Drive up Mountain Road for 0.4 mile to the parking area on your left.

The park is open from sunrise to one-half hour after sunset. The park office is open Thursday through Monday, 8:00 A.M. to 4:00 P.M. The Summit House is open 11:30 A.M. to 5:30 P.M., Saturday, Sunday, and holidays, weather permitting. There is no fee to park at the lower parking area abutting Mountain Road; no parking is allowed here between 8:00 P.M. and 8:00 A.M. Rest rooms are located under the porch on the north side of the Summit House; a portable toilet is located on the Halfway House grounds. Dogs must be leashed, and trash must be packed out.

—R.L.

Holyoke Range State Park
Amherst/Granby
2,252 acres

- **2.75 miles**
- **3 hours**
- **moderate**

Somewhat surprisingly, it is not the better known Mt. Holyoke but Mt. Norwottock (1,106 feet) that is the highest point of the six-mile-long Holyoke Range. Formed by two major lava flows some 200 million years ago, the basaltic spine of the Holyoke Range is unusual in that it is one of only a relatively few east-west ranges in America and the largest in Massachusetts. The Connecticut River flows through a water gap in the erosion-resistant rock here—a gap that separates this range from the similar Mt. Tom Range on the west side of the river.

Holyoke Range State Park offers an extensive trail system through attractive birch/oak/maple woodlands leading to several promontories with beautiful views. The 117-mile Metacomet-Monadnock Trail (M-M Trail) follows the ridge line and connects the park with adjacent Skinner State Park and Mt. Holyoke (see p. 215) about 3 miles to the west. Picturesque rock overhangs known as Horse Caves are said to have sheltered the revolutionary-era tax protester Daniel Shays and his men and horses. Route 116, running through a gap in the range called the Notch, was originally a trail used by Native Americans; now Notch Visitor Center, on the east side of the road, is the gateway to this popular park and its trails.

The route described below will take you eastward from the visitor center to the somewhat open summit of Mt. Norwottock by way of the M-M Trail (some distant views are possible before you reach the summit of Mt.

Norwottock); down and up slightly to and through a large split boulder and the Horse Caves; down and up again to the summit of Rattlesnake Knob (813 feet elevation), where you'll appreciate the splendid panoramic view; and then back to the visitors center by way of Southside Trail. The trails are well marked and quite well maintained thanks in large measure to the Friends of the Holyoke Range. Some trails traverse private property.

After parking in the large paved lot, you may wish to enter the visitor center to view exhibits and obtain a map and additional information about current trail conditions. Rest rooms are available. Follow the orange, white, and blue paint blazes from behind the center (called Laurel Loop) and cross the gravel road (once an old trolley bed). Follow the Metacomet-Monadnock and Robert Frost Trails (follow orange and white blazes) when they jog left, then right over the road. Cross a cleared utility line right-of-way where birds that prefer edge habitats, such as rufous-sided towhee (listen for its well-known "drink-your-tea" song), gray catbird, and, in the wetter spots, common yellowthroat, reside.

Pass near a rock quarry, where basalt is mined, on the right (notice that the trails here are littered with iron-rich basalt that produces a characteristic metallic clinking sound as you knock them about while walking). Follow the white blazes as the M-M Trail bears right (Robert Frost Trail continues straight). A private shooting range is located just north of the visitor center, and the constant firing can be a great distraction as you wend your way up the slopes toward Mt. Norwottock. Fortunately, the sounds will eventually diminish and then disappear altogether as you continue eastward. Mt. Greylock, the state's highest peak, is already visible (38 miles to the northwest) from a point left of the trail well before the summit. In the foreground is the rounded mass of Bare Mountain, just west of Route 116.

Northern red oaks and blue jays, which feast upon the bitter acorns, predominate on these lower slopes. Wildflowers such as heart-leaved aster, which blooms white in late summer; false Solomon's seal; and Canada mayflower are very common forms on the forest floor. The trail ascends rather steeply at times and enters a moister zone where sugar maple is the most common tree. Christmas fern, an indicator of rich, organic soils, provides color here even in winter. The trail then drops before rising to the summit and a red metal observation tower. The lower steps have been removed so climbing the tower is not encouraged. However, the views from the solid bedrock near the tower are stunning.

The view of Amherst, less than 5 miles to the north, is nice but there's an even better view to the east from the outcrop just below the tower, to the right of the trail. The observation tower at Quabbin Reservoir is also visible 17 miles away to the east. On a sunny day, bask in the sun on the warm basalt, as we did. Stunted oaks, low-bush blueberry, hairgrass (with very thin leaves), and little bluestem grass have taken foothold on the sunny, rocky summit. From here you may also see **broad-winged hawks** and **turkey vultures** riding the warm thermals that are deflected up the mountainside.

The trail now descends past basalt outcrops, through a narrow cleft formed by a house-sized boulder that has broken in two, to the formation known as the **Horse Caves** 0.2 mile from the Mt. Norwottock summit.

*The Metacomet-
Monadnock Trail
passes through a
narrow crevice in a
split boulder just above
the ledge overhang
known as Horse Caves.*

The caves actually were created when sandstone and conglomerate, a sedimentary rock made of rock fragments cemented together, broke away leaving a protective overhang. A pair of eastern phoebes (a member of the flycatcher family) apparently have found the stone ceiling suitable for attaching their mud nest. Phoebe nests always have an exterior layer of green moss decorating them—perhaps for camouflage?

Follow the trail downhill to the right where it skirts the bottom of a rock slide (talus slope). The basalt making up this ridge is 600 feet thick. Ages of freezing and thawing have worked loose the chunks of rust-stained basalt along their characteristic hexagonal cleavage planes—with gravity doing the rest. The trail passes through dry, sunny, semiopen deciduous woodland of oak, laurel, blueberry, azalea, and witch hazel in the level area between summits.

Your next destination is Rattlesnake Knob. Bear right at the intersection, then bear left a few hundred feet farther along where the blue-blazed Southside Trail goes right. Bear right where Robert Frost Trail intersects the combined M-M and Robert Frost Trails (marked with white, yellow, and orange blazes). The trail ascends moderately to the right; go right at the next split in the trail. Pass a red metal town boundary marker with **A** on one side for Amherst and **G** on the other for Granby.

Pignut hickory, northern red oak, and red maple are the dominant woody vegetation on these slopes. Stay left at the trail junction and walk a short distance uphill to the viewpoint on Rattlesnake Knob (elevation 813 feet). The chances of seeing a rattlesnake here are slim to none; more likely you might encounter the ubiquitous common garter snake sunning itself at the edge of the trail. All snakes play a vital role of keeping prey populations in check but are often unfairly maligned. A beautiful panorama of green rolling hills, including the diagonal ridge of Long Mountain, is laid out before you. Small red cedar trees (actually juniper) and shrub-sized **dwarf oak** with shiny, dark green leaves grow on this southeast-facing rocky outcrop. Listen for the guttural croaks of soaring ravens, or watch the comings and goings of insects on the rocks at your feet. On a visit in September we witnessed a small drama unfold as we watched a tiny ant's single-minded struggle to drag away a much larger and heavier bronze-colored beetle.

To begin your return hike, walk back down from the Knob and turn left at the combined M-M and Robert Frost Trails (orange and white blazes). Walk down a rather steep, rocky slope where Christmas fern grows rather abundantly. Three-tenths of one mile below the summit you'll come to a junction with Cliffside Trail, also a bridle trail, blazed with red paint. Turn right onto this wide track and pass through a shady hemlock grove. Soon smooth, light-gray-trunked American beech trees outnumber all others. Many species of birds and mammals feed on the beech's nutritious three-sided seeds, which are enclosed in prickly capsules. Continue on through a small area of dead timber just before the next trail intersection.

A dried vernal pool is situated on the right at the intersection with the blue-blazed Southside Trail. Dry when we visited, this pool holds water in spring and early summer. Wood frogs and spotted and Jefferson salamanders make overland migrations to court and breed here. They must complete their breeding cycles before the pool dries up in late summer. Follow the Southside Trail straight ahead for about 2,000 feet and cross one of the few streams that carries water year-round on the southern flank of the range. It is an oasis for amphibians like the small green and brown pickerel frog. Do not drink the water, however, as most streams in Massachusetts are contaminated by the parasite *Giardia lamblia*.

Almost immediately after crossing the brook, turn right briefly onto the red- and blue-blazed Swamp/

Southside Trail. The trail splits and you'll want to take the blue-blazed Southside Trail left to where it meets Lower Access Trail (this area is somewhat confusing relative to the state park map). Stay right at the next intersection (if you turn left, you'll cross a stream) and continue west on the Southside Trail. Later, cross a dry brook bed in the oak/maple woods and walk gradually uphill. Odd-looking **squawroot** pokes up through the leaf litter under the oaks here. It looks something like an inverted pinecone with brownish scales and yellowish flowers that bloom in spring. Squawroot is a parasite lacking chlorophyll and must draw nourishment from the oak roots.

The trail then enters drier white pine/oak forest with a shrub layer of highbush blueberry (an indicator of acidic soil) and mountain laurel. At the next intersection, stay right on the blue-blazed Southside Trail (a sign at the intersection indicates the direction of the visitor center). Walk uphill to the junction with the M-M Trail; turn left, then right after about 50 feet. Follow the M-M Trail back to the junction with the Robert Frost Trail and turn left on it. Cross the road and follow the Laurel Loop back to the Notch Visitor Center.

Getting There

Take Route 116 north from the center of South Hadley for 4.5 miles to the Notch Visitor Center parking area on the right. There is a sign for the center on Route 116.

From Route 9 in Amherst, travel south on Route 116 for 5.1 miles to the visitor center on the left. After leaving your locked vehicle, walk left and then left again up the stairs to the big, modern brick and stone building that has wildlife exhibits, maps, and rest rooms.

Trail hours are dawn to dusk. Visitor center hours are Thursday through Monday, 8:00 A.M. to 4:00 P.M. Signs tell visitors not to leave valuables in their cars and not to drink the water in streams. Dogs are allowed but must be kept on leashes. The park is popular with mountain bikers as well as hikers. Motor vehicles are prohibited. Since some trails cross private property, be sure not to stray off the trails.

—R.L.

Mt. Tom State Reservation
Holyoke/Easthampton
1,683 acres

- **4.5 miles**
- **4 hours**
- **difficult**

A colleague, whose given name coincidentally is Tom, grew up in the shadow of the mountain he always identified with so strongly—becoming a nationally known expert in the field of herpetology (the study of scaly [reptiles] and slimy [amphibians] vertebrates) in the process. Perhaps fittingly, Mt. Tom is one of the last strongholds of the eastern timber rattlesnake and copperhead, both endangered species.

This north-south trending **volcanic spine,** separated from the east-west Holyoke Range by the broad, meandering Connecticut River, has an extensive trail network, including the Metacomet-Monadnock (M-M) Trail. Ponds and wetlands, including vernal pools, extensive oak/hickory forests, and **breathtaking views** provide hours of wonderful hiking and nature study. You'll want to return again and again to explore the variety of natural communities encompassed by the reservation.

Scorching lava flows, welling to the surface some 200 million years ago, solidified to form the rusty basalt columns that we see today in the Mt. Tom and Holyoke

Mt. Tom State Reservation

(closed in winter)

East St.

Christopher Clark Rd.

Basalt Tower

M-M Trail

glacial erratic

Tote Rd.

Kay Bee Tr.

lost boulder

Bray Brook

Quarry Tr.

Bray Loop Tr.

Lake Bray

Route 91

Smiths Ferry Rd.

Mt. Tom

N

2000 feet

Ranges. Thought to have been named for an early seventeenth-century English explorer, Rowland Thomas, Mt. Tom forms a resistant monolith towering 1,100 feet above the mighty river that served as the "highway" for Rowland and other early colonists. Industry, agriculture, and, later, higher education continue to be prominent bulwarks of the valley economy. Mt. Tom State Reservation, one of the state's oldest, was established in 1903.

This round-trip walk begins at a picnic pavilion at the intersection of Smiths Ferry and Christopher Clark Roads across from reservation headquarters, where there is ample parking available. Walk southeast along paved Smiths Ferry Road for 0.1 mile and cross the road to join the white-blazed M-M Trail on the left. A map of the entire 117-mile trail is located here. Pass a building on the left and walk through a stand of big, tall red oaks and eastern hemlocks. Tiny, energetic golden-crowned kinglets search the conifer boughs for insects and other invertebrates. They are usually located here, first in spring and fall, by their high-pitched, sibilant calls. The trail is fairly flat and wide as it passes through red maples, hemlocks, and American chestnut sprouts. Tufted titmice, attractive, gray-crested birds with peachy flanks, are year-round residents that whistle "peter, peter, peter."

After about 10 minutes you'll arrive at Quarry Trail junction; a Department of Environmental Management (DEM) maintenance/storage area is on the right. From

Glacial ice planed off the top of the landmark basalt tower which stands above Easthampton on Mt. Tom's precipitous west face.

here it's 2 miles on the M-M Trail to the Mt. Tom summit. This is where the real walking begins as you head up rather steeply, via one switchback, to a partially screened vantage point. The Connecticut River Oxbow (cut off by the river circa 1830) and I-91 to the north will be visible to the right. Scaly, pink-trunked red pines grow on this slope. They have long, paired needles. The next overlook from the ledge is more open. From here the state's highest point—Mt. Greylock—is visible as a bump 33 miles to the northwest. Easthampton lies directly below you.

The basalt rock hints at its high iron content with its rusty exterior and the metallic clinking sound it makes as you knock pieces together. The path winds up through a crevice in an outcrop adorned by **mountain ash** shrubs. Not an ash at all, in autumn they produce large clusters of bright red berries. This fruit, along with its yellow foliage, when seen against the azure blue of the sky is truly lovely. Robins, cedar waxwings, and other fruit eaters can make quick work of the offering. Oak woods now become prominent, and evergreen wood fern grows in blue-green clumps among the rocks.

The trail levels out for stretches, skirting the summit of Whiting Peak (1,010 feet) to the left, allowing you to pay more attention to the woodland asters blooming as white stars in fall. Watch for migrant birds; flickers display their bright yellow underwing linings as they shoot past. After proceeding 0.7 mile from the Quarry Trail junction, reach the two D.O.C. Trail junctions, left, which are blazed in red. Climb up and over a low rock outcrop on the left covered with mountain ash. The rock below forms a sort of "pavement" with the hexagonal cleavage planes of the basalt clearly visible.

As I walked this trail on a splendid sunny day in mid-October, a big black raven, perched on the ledge up ahead, launched itself off the cliff. These rocky crags are favorite perches. **Ravens** are much larger than crows and, in fact, weigh about four times more than their smaller relative. I always enjoy seeing these magnificent birds.

Proceeding now over barren rock where rectangular white blazes are painted directly on ledges, you'll catch your first glimpse of one of the many communications antennas situated on the ridge. Little bluestem grass and abundant stiff aster, with heads of violet flowers, grow on the dry, exposed outcrops. It's difficult to imagine that a mile-thick sheet of ice once rode up and over this basalt ridge, yet clear evidence rests just "off" the trail. Take a sharp turn to the right and downhill at a six-foot-long glacial erratic. This boulder is clearly composed of a rock other than basalt. The ice carried this hunk of granite southward some 12,000 years ago.

A clump of small but picturesque gray birches greets you with waving long, pointed yellow leaves as you walk down and approach the precipice. The footing is quite good, but be careful. Model railroaders will recognize reindeer moss, a silvery green lichen that is processed and used to create trees and shrubs on a miniature scale. The path then reenters woods of oak, red maple, chestnut, witch hazel, and blueberry. Turning over logs, as I often do in a search for salamanders, I found two individuals of the red-backed species in a low damp spot left of the trail and then carefully replaced them under their protective log shelters.

The way in which this hardened lava fractures is very convenient for the hiker. The rock forms natural staircases that are a pleasure to walk up or down. The M-M Trail drops below the antennas to the left. Nearby to the right is a landmark **basalt tower,** which is reminiscent of a huge petrified tree stump. Proceed up over outcrops but be heartened by the good footing. Among the rocks grow pussytoes and meadowsweet. Bush clover, a member of the pea family, grows about two feet tall on these sunny outcrops, producing seeds eaten by birds such as white-throated sparrows. From here, you'll be able to see Mt. Monadnock (the terminus of the M-M Trail), 50 miles away to the northeast. **Huckleberry thickets** full of burgundy red leaves enliven the sunny outcrops, and in the low woodlands, patches of maple-leaf viburnum glow with an unusual and beautiful rosé wine color.

Scrub oak and sweet fern, both indicators of dry, sandy soils, provide shrubby cover here. The crushed foliage and twigs of sweet fern—not a fern at all—are very fragrant. Wild roses along the path produce red, seed-filled "hips" in late summer. Below the second communications tower a windmill was erected in the fall of 1994 by the University of Massachusetts. It is supplying 20 percent of the electricity needed to light the trails of the nearby ski area (the equivalent of power for 40 homes). This idea caused me to reflect upon the merits of providing energy from renewable sources versus the desire to keep such scenic summits safe from development.

Continue straight at a major rock crevice on the left. This is an area of short-stature oak woods providing the first clear view of the Mt. Tom summit antenna farm. Alternating ups and downs lead you between outcrops that provide stunning views to the west and of the Mt. Tom massif itself. The summit is marred by development. A metal fence with Danger High Level Radiation and No Trespassing signs surrounds the antennas. Not a pretty sight. The M-M Trail continues down to the ski area and beyond, but this is the turnaround point for this walk—one and one-half hours out from the Quarry Trail junction and 1,200 feet above sea level.

If you're like me, you'll want to get away from this "developed" area as quickly as possible. Return back down the trail, as I did, and find a great spot to have lunch and survey the countryside. As I relaxed, a raven flew by—doing flips—legs down and generally cavorting. Bearberry, I've found, grows on some of the exposed outcrops. This low-growing evergreen member of the heath family is usually associated more with the dune lands of Cape Cod than with the hills of western Massachusetts—but here it is.

Two adult red-tailed hawks (fully adult birds have red tails but immatures don't) circled overhead near the cliff, riding the warm up-drafts. Among the oaks growing here are red, white, black, and a little bit of scrub oak, which never attains tree size. Other species of birds may come into view, including big **turkey vultures** that sail just below and parallel with the top of the cliff. As I walked that day, I was struck by how really gorgeous the fall foliage was. It was one of those days when you think: "How great it is to be alive!"

Returning, you reach the two D.O.C. Trail junctions on the right. (If you wish to vary your return, take the second D.O.C. Trail 0.9 mile to Quarry Trail and then take Quarry Trail 0.3 mile back to the M-M Trail at the maintenance/storage area.)

If continuing on the M-M Trail, watch for trailing arbutus (a May bloomer) and spotted wintergreen, which has attractive dark green and white leaves. You may also notice a few low azaleas and some white, wax-like Indian pipes—parasitic flowering plants containing no chlorophyll. After about one and one-half hours of leisurely walking from the summit, reach the Quarry Trail intersection. Continue straight and follow it back through the oaks and hemlocks to Smiths Ferry Road. Turn left, cross the road, and walk back down to the picnic pavilion and parking area.

Getting There

From Springfield, take I-91 north to Exit 17A (Route 141). Reach Route 5 (which is not mentioned on the exit sign) in 0.3 mile. Turn left at the traffic light and drive 3.9 miles on Route 5 to Smiths Ferry Road. The entrance to the reservation is on the left. If traveling south on I-91, take Exit 18, turn right at Route 5, and follow it south for approximately 3.2 miles to Smiths Ferry Road on the right. Pass under I-91 as you drive up Smiths Ferry Road into the reservation and reach a contact station. From here, continue 1.6 miles on Smiths Ferry Road, past Bray Lake on the left, to the pavilion and picnic area at the junction of Christopher Clark and Smiths Ferry Roads.

Hours are 8:00 A.M. to sunset; gates are locked until 8:00 A.M. Daily parking fee is two dollars per vehicle. Motorized vehicles and mountain bikes prohibited from trails; hunting not allowed. The rest room building at Bray Lake picnic area is open Memorial Day to Labor Day. A chemical toilet is also present.

—R.L.

Sanderson Brook Falls
Chester/Blandford
2,308 acres

- **2 miles**
- **2 hours**
- **easy**

The cold clear waters of Sanderson Brook, a tributary of the Westfield River, gush over vertically contorted rock strata, creating a single dramatic drop as well as alternating pools and cascades in an idyllic woodland setting. Beautiful Sanderson Brook Falls, perhaps 75 feet high in all, is certainly the most notable feature of Chester-Blandford State Forest. Sculpted by three brook systems, the property in northwest Hampden County borders the nearly pristine West Branch of the Westfield River, a major tributary of the mighty Connecticut. In 1994 the Westfield became the first river in Massachusetts to receive National Wild and Scenic River status.

Streams and pools provide ideal conditions for several species of aquatic and semiaquatic salamanders. The woods are home to red-backed salamanders—the most abundant vertebrate (by biomass) in the eastern forests—as well as some of the most accomplished avian songsters in the woodlands: winter wren, Louisiana waterthrush, and hermit thrush. The first two have loud songs designed to be heard above the sound of flowing

240   Hampshire and Hampden Counties

Sanderson Brook Falls

Westfield River

Route 20

P

rest rooms
kiosk

Sanderson Brook

Griffin Brook Rd.

Sanderson
Brook Falls

Observation Hill Rd.

N

1250 feet

water. Listen also for the robinlike phrases of the brilliant, but easily overlooked, **scarlet tanager** in the deciduous woods. It is one of many woodland species that spends the bulk of its year in the rapidly shrinking tropical forests of northern South America, flying north to mate and raise its young.

From the dirt parking area walk up the gradually climbing dirt road. The park map shows a hiking trail paralleling the stream but this trail is difficult, if not impossible, to locate at present. Walk along the north-west-facing slope of a shaded hemlock gorge cut by the modest yet relentless waters of Sanderson Brook, with a steep hillside on the left. Dusky and two-lined salamanders live in the wet environment along the stream edges. Neither has lungs; instead, they breathe through their moist, sticky skins. Head upstream, climbing progressively higher above the brook. Beside hemlock and yellow birch—my favorite among the hardwoods (I love the fine, peely quality of its golden metallic bark)— you'll also find red maple, sugar maple, northern red oak, American beech, basswood, and smooth-trunked (except the oldest) black birch.

The understory includes witch hazel, striped maple (a.k.a., moosewood, goosefoot maple), and mountain maple—which produces reddish, winged seeds in summer. Here and there are thickets of hobblebush and American yew, which looks a good deal like another of its common names—ground hemlock. In summer, **red-flowering raspberry** is studded with attractive roselike blossoms that will catch your eye. The deep shade below the hemlocks is not conducive to wildflower growth, but in summer you may find the greenish white shinleaf, whorled loosestrife (a yellow-blossomed plant that favors moist ground), and clusters of ghostly white Indian pipes, a flowering plant that lacks chlorophyll. The nodding pipes become more erect with age. In May you'll find blooming clintonia and Canada mayflower (both lilies), wild sarsaparilla, starflower, partridgeberry, and the lovely red-and-white painted trillium.

After about 20 minutes of walking, come to a bridge over Sanderson Brook. The bridge is closed to traffic, but many people drive to this point and begin their walk here. Cross the bridge (note the rocky/gravelly bottom of the streambed—the swift flow washing finer particles downstream), and after a short distance cross the brook again and continue walking up the road toward the falls. After another 15 minutes of walking, look for a well-worn path on the right that goes down the slope toward the base of the falls. It should take you only 2 minutes to reach it from the road.

In July, the cool breezes from the falls are welcome relief from the heat. A luxuriant growth of mosses and less familiar **liverworts** drape the damp rocks, while the vertically tilted and layered bedrock surrounding the falls is capped by dark green hemlocks. Odd nonflowering plants, liverworts grow tonguelike on wet rock surfaces among the mosses. Predatory water striders skate across the surface film of the pools. (To take photos of this fairyland scene, given the dimly lit conditions, I recommend film speeds of ASA 200 or higher or using a tripod.) Even in midsummer the volume of water is quite considerable. The soothing sound of flowing water is sure to lower your stress level. You'll doubtless want to rock-hop across the brook to clamber up along the left side of the falls for a closer look at the alternating pour-offs and pools, but watch your footing.

The sunny clearing below the falls provides the right conditions for the orange trumpets of spotted touch-me-

The falls plunge in a single dramatic drop plus alternating cascades and pools for a total distance of about 75 vertical feet.

not, a favorite of ruby-throated hummingbirds. Pink joe-pye weed and white-flowering boneset—once used medicinally—also thrive here. Moisture-loving sensitive and interrupted ferns, as well as primitive soda-straw-shaped horsetails grow here, too. Bush honeysuckle, in contrast, shows off its yellow blossoms in summer from the dry, gravelly slopes above the brook.

Broken glass and other debris are unfortunately an unwelcome sight detracting from an otherwise sublime setting. After spending time at the falls, you may want to walk to a lookout site along the road, above the falls, before returning to your vehicle. To reach it, return to Sanderson Brook Road on the same path and turn right. You'll soon reach a spot where, to the right (west), you can gaze through a gap in the canopy toward the falls. A wooded ridge is visible rising up behind the falls.

To further explore the hemlock stands above and south of the falls, follow the road up another 2,000 feet to a bridge (that is out) over Sanderson Brook. Follow the brook downstream over informal trails and then swing right, downhill, and then uphill back to the road. This area is laced with all-terrain-vehicle tracks but offers some spectacular views from ledges under the hemlocks down into the rocky gorge. After rejoining the road, turn left and head back to your vehicle.

Getting There

From the intersection of Routes 20 and 112 in the center of Huntington, travel west for 4.3 miles and turn left onto Sanderson Brook Road (there is a brown, wooden Forest and Parks sign on the left for Sanderson Brook Falls at this point). The dirt parking area is located on the right, 0.15 mile from the Route 20 turnoff.

Hours are dawn to dusk. There is no fee for hikers. Motorized vehicles are prohibited. Trail maps are available from the kiosk situated at the end of the camp- ground loop road, located on the left, off Route 20, approximately 1.0 mile before Sanderson Brook Road. Rest rooms are also located here.

—R.L.

Tolland State Forest
Tolland/Blandford/Otis/Sandisfield
9,000 acres

- 3.3 miles
- 3 hours
- moderate

Because of its elevation atop the undulating Southern Berkshire Plateau, the woodlands of Tolland State Forest are dominated by northern hardwoods. But Otis Reservoir, one of the largest water bodies in western Massachusetts at 1,000 acres, forms the focal point for numerous anglers, hunters, campers, off-road-vehicle users, and others who visit. The trail system is little used by hikers—quite a contrast to the heavily utilized recreation areas—making a sojourn to this property, which imparts a wilderness feeling, rewarding and enjoyable.

After parking in a large paved lot, just before the contact station, walk south to the entrance of Gilmore Trail (no sign) in the direction of the reservoir. Pass the Gilmore Trail exit first (this will be your return point) to reach the outbound trailhead approximately 50 feet farther; turn left onto the trail. Follow it a very short distance and turn right at the first junction. The trail is marked by triangular blue plastic markers (some with a bear track symbol) and older painted blue blazes.

Tolland State Forest

Otis Reservoir

Southwest Bay

CCC Tr.

Larson Tr.

Sawmill Tr.

East Otis Rd.

Gilmore Trail

Alan Rd.

contact station

Hall Rd.

Southeast Bay

Lair Mtn.

Belden Rd.

N

1000 feet

Breathe in the wonderful earthy fragrances of this rich, moist forest of American beech; eastern hemlock; and yellow, black, and white birches. The understory contains mountain laurel and tiny clubmosses—princess pine (also known as tree clubmoss), ground cedar, and shining clubmosses. These attractive evergreen plants spread by underground runners and by minute, dustlike spores borne by candlelike structures. Goldthread, a wetland indicator that is common here under the hemlocks, has shiny green three-parted leaves and starry white flowers in May. Hermit thrushes skulk in the shade, uttering their beautiful flutelike songs at dusk. The trail climbs modestly and then enters a white pine stand of medium age. Eastern white pine (also known as old field white pine) is a colonizer of abandoned farmland—forming thick, rather even-aged stands. Stone walls tell of a time when this ground provided forage for pasturing livestock.

After passing through a sugar maple stand, cross dirt East Otis Road, and find the first sign for Gilmore Trail. Descend through woodland ever so slightly and come to the border of a mowed field—perhaps 1.5 acres—on your right. Walk out into the field and examine the plants and insects, including butterflies, crickets, and grasshoppers. Common flickers frequent open habitats and search for ants by probing their long, stout bills into ant nests in the ground. Openings like these in otherwise closed forest have a special appeal for me. The blue sky is unobstructed, and the warm sunshine on my face always seems to improve my disposition. In early fall watch for hawks, migrating monarch butterflies, and other airborne creatures.

Smooth silvery beech trunks, red maples, and white pines define the woods as you return to the trail, which soon makes a sharp left. A large gray boulder on the right has a white quartz vein vertically bisecting it. Quartz is a very hard mineral from which sand grains are made. Even after the bulk of the boulder has worn away, the quartz will probably remain. Shade-tolerant hemlocks—from whose reddish inner bark tannin (used in the leather tanning process) originates—become numerous on the slope that drops off to the right (west).

Soon you'll reach a spring. Water flows through a red clay pipe that has been sealed in by cemented stones to protect the spring from contamination, but it is recommended that you not drink untreated water such as this. Large yellow birches—the trees with peely, metallic bark—provide solitary vireos with nest sites and nesting material. Vireos build cup-shaped nests in the fork of a branch, weaving thin birch bark strips (usually paper or white birch) into the nest. The trail skirts the top of a fairly old beech/hemlock stand with little understory or ground cover and ascends gradually to some rather large black birches. The sap contains oil of wintergreen. The familiar aroma of this fragrant oil will delight your nose if you break a twig and sniff it.

Just before you reach Sawmill Trail (a wood road used by ORVs), encounter a small fern glade and the remnants of an old stone wall. Hay-scented fern is partial to sun-dappled rocky pastures—as this once was. Now, in mid-September, its fronds were already turning yellow. Hidden beneath your feet, hairy-tailed moles "swim" through the soil seeking—by touch and smell— worms, grubs, and other soil invertebrates. Coming only rarely to the surface, these creatures have dark gray, plush, reversible fur that facilitates their movement— forward or backward. Aboveground all that betrays their presence is a raised ribbon of soil and an occasional mound of earth.

Pick up Gilmore Trail again after crossing Sawmill Trail. Cross an intermittent streambed. After crossing another wood road—this one obviously heavily used by off-road vehicles—enter an attractive forest of mostly gray and black birches, with some hemlock and beech. An increasing number of blowdowns on this portion of the trail makes it a bit more difficult to navigate. Middle-aged and moderately large red oaks now become much more common. Oaks are among the latest trees to change color in fall—generally turning yellowish and coppery hues. Boulders of gneiss and schist protrude from the forest floor. The wavy lines of the schist show distortions caused by incredible heat and pressure.

Striped maples increase in abundance below the canopy formed by the beech trees. Most of the beeches show signs of fungal disease that cause rough, bumpy lesions in the bark. Beeches reproduce by vigorous sprouting, and large trees are often surrounded by a thicket of small-diameter offspring. The delicious nuts are eaten by many mammals and birds. Black cherry trees also increase in number. Unlike beeches, cherries are very intolerant of shading and, in fact, are among the first trees to colonize abandoned fields along with pines and gray birches. The brown, hulking skeletons of ancient sugar maples stand erect just before the trail crosses hard-surfaced Alan Road and continues in a southeasterly direction (Gilmore Trail is indicated by signs in both directions).

The trail leads through damp ground populated by sensitive fern (sensitive to frost) and horsetails. The tracks of white-tailed deer show clearly in the damp, dark earth. After passing through an open wet area thick with ferns, the trail passes through a stand of tall white pines. Woodpeckers flake off the bark of dead trees to expose fat, juicy beetle grubs, and red-breasted nuthatches creep along, surveying bark crevices for spiders and insects. This area is somewhat overgrown and brushy with a thick growth of sapling black birches; young trees possess a dark, shiny, tight-fitting bark marked by small horizontal corky growths called lenticels that admit air. You'll find white ashes and white pines growing in the next damp open area. White ashes do well in moist ground and produce winged seeds that resemble canoe paddles. Their trunks tend to be tall and straight.

After crossing a stone wall the trail passes through low forest and then through a planted Norway spruce stand to reach East Otis Road. Beneath the dark, towering alien spruces the ground is littered with the large "cores" of spruce cones that have been stripped of their scales by **red squirrels** in order to reach the luscious seeds beneath. These small, seemingly hyperactive squirrels eagerly take advantage of these non-natives within their midst. On the east side of the road the trail descends gradually and heads northerly through woodland of beech, birch, and maple. Their usual associate—eastern hemlock—occupies the shaded and damp spots like the one ahead.

A small stream flows through the stand and feeds the wetland to the right, an extension of Dismal Bay at the extreme southern end of the reservoir. A bit of searching beneath the flat stones of the two brooks here may produce a three-inch-long two-lined salamander. After gently examining the bronzy yellow stripe down its back, return it to the stream. On warm damp evenings these amphibians are sometimes found foraging well away from water.

There was already some color in the swamp—the red maples—during my mid-September visit. A native holly, **winterberry,** grows along this wetland edge. A low, conifer-studded ridge that borders the far edge of the wetland beckons, but it is out of reach. Gingerly working my way around the standing water and through the thick vegetation, I was able to locate beaver-cut red maples quite close to the trail. A pickerel frog leaped to safety as I clambered about.

Gilmore Trail then climbs gradually away from the wetland through hemlock and beech, then sugar maples,

Winterberry, a native holly that grows in wet places and loses its leaves in fall, provides birds with a feast of bright red berries during winter.

and again more hemlock. Here the trail makes a sharp left turn—the one spot where losing the route is a distinct possibility as a few downed trees obscure the trail. Follow the trail slightly up over rocks through a forest of young beech, sugar maple, and hemlock. The crest of a ridge drops off to the right. These rocky beech woods contain thick growths of beechdrops. These six-inch plants lack chlorophyll and are parasitic on beech roots; in autumn they produce small whitish flowers flecked with purple.

Pass a large rotting sugar maple, right, as the trail climbs gradually. The peace and quiet were palpable here—no human-made sounds were audible as I walked along enjoying the day. I heard the "peeps" of six **spring peepers** calling that mid-September day. Where the trail splits, follow the right fork downhill toward the lake. The old red paint trail blazes are difficult to see here. The trail leads under hemlock trees and over fern-covered rocks.

Continue downhill. The blue plastic blazes resume, and soon the blue waters of Otis Reservoir come into view on your right. The path will take you to the shore and then parallel it. The reservoir was created in 1866 when the Fall River, a tributary of the Farmington, was dammed; the dam was reinforced with granite blocks in 1888. The State Forest was established in 1924. During the 1930s the Civilian Conservation Corps (CCC) constructed many of the facilities. Hobblebush grows thickly near the shore, and a few small native red spruces are also to be found here. I was fortunate to spy a **pied-billed grebe** riding low in the water; it soon disappeared—only to reappear 50 feet farther away 30 seconds later. No doubt it was a migrant. These small grebes are rare and declining freshwater marsh breeders in Massachusetts. Among the most primitive of birds, grebes are nearly helpless on shore since their aft-mounted legs make walking extremely difficult; in the water they are superb divers.

Across Southeast Bay is Lair Mountain (1,674 feet), its fire tower clearly visible. After swinging briefly away from the shore, the trail returns to it amid a forest of beech and hemlock, with hobblebush beneath. It produces bouquets of small white flowers in May. The trail soon emerges from the woods at the parking area where the walk originated.

Getting There

From the intersection of Routes 5 and 20 in West Springfield, take Route 20 west through Westfield for 17.5 miles to Route 23 in Woronoco and turn left onto Route 23. Drive west on Route 23 for 12.0 miles through Blandford to Reservoir Road in Otis on the left. Turn left onto Reservoir Road and drive west to Tolland Road (the third road on the left). Turn onto Tolland Road and drive south along the shore; stay right where Kibbe Road goes left. Continue south to the road leading to the contact station and campground—turn left at this intersection.

Hours are dawn to dusk. No fees to walk. No toilets located at contact station/public boat ramp. Camping available—reservations can be made. No hunting or trapping of birds and mammals allowed.

—R.L.

Granville State Forest
Granville/Tolland
2,397 acres

- **2 miles**
- **3 hours**
- **moderate**

Though far from being wilderness, this property is suffi-
ciently isolated to give a sense of tranquil remoteness.
My wife, Chris, and I felt it during one visit in early September. Perhaps the warm rays of the late summer sun
imparted a feeling of peace and utter relaxation as we
lingered along the shores of an unnamed pond—its bordering meadows thick with blooming goldenrod.

Granville State Forest lies in Hampden County; its
southern boundary abuts the state of Connecticut. Like
much of New England, this land was once the domain of
sheep and dairy cows. It is slowly reverting back to
northern hardwood forest. This regeneration has created
a rich mix of natural and seminatural communities
where wildlife viewing can be excellent. Hints of former
human occupation remain, such as an old apple orchard
and horticultural plantings at an abandoned homesite
along West Hartland Road.

This loop walk will take you along gurgling brooks,
through woodlands rich in wildflowers to an artificial
pond, past the old homesite, alongside a wild beaver

Granville State Forest

N

1/4 mile

Miller Rd.

Hubbard Brook

Halfway Brook

rock ledge

P

beaver
pond

West Hartland Rd.

dam
pond

Hartland Rd.

Pipeline R.O.W.

flowage under towering pines, and back to your car.
Endowed with a fine reptile and amphibian population,
Granville is also a wonderful place to look for mammals

256   Hampshire and Hampden Counties

and their signs. Coyote, red fox, raccoon, beaver, and numerous smaller creatures abound. Woodland and wetland birds are abundant also. Old fields and meadows of flowering plants host bees, butterflies, beetles, and other winged insects.

The trail begins on the east side of West Hartland Road adjacent to an attractive millpond flanked by eastern hemlock, white pine, and red maple. During migration, these trees may be full of colorful warblers, vireos, and other birds. Just north of the pond is a camping area. After parking in a turnout along the opposite side of the road, cross the road diagonally to the right and follow the trail around the right of the millpond; a wooden bridge over the spillway connects the trail to the camping area; do not cross the bridge. The faded blue triangular blazes are difficult to see but the trail is fairly easy to locate. Walk through dimly lit hemlock woods on a soft, needle-cushioned path.

At times, the trail climbs slightly above Halfway Brook in a small hemlock gorge. Note a 10-foot rock ledge on the left near the stream. Less than one-half mile from the start, arrive at a **lovely little falls.** Dusky and two-lined salamanders live in the moist environment along the shoreline and under flat stones. Both lack lungs, absorbing oxygen directly through their mucous-covered skins into their bloodstreams. A common ground cover here is the fragrant (if you crush a leaf or red berry) wintergreen, whose shiny oval leaves stay green year-round, as the name implies. (Fast film or a tripod is required to photograph in the dim light.)

Just before you reach Hubbard Brook you'll come to a small wet clearing. The trail continues as a narrow grassy path on the right, climbing up the moderately steep hillside along a Tenneco natural gas pipeline right-of-way. Take a look at attractive Hubbard Brook (which can be crossed on stepping-stones at low flow) before proceeding up the right-of-way, bordered by hemlock forest. Climb almost 250 feet, to an elevation of 1,240 feet. From here look back toward Hubbard Brook for a rather nice view of the forested ridge on the north side of the stream.

After the path peaks, it dips slightly and becomes wet. Brown-blotched pickerel frogs jump suddenly at your approach as you step through the drainage swale. Climbing again, reaching a stand of large white pines on the true crest, look for a wide trail marked with new blue blazes on the right. The air is filled with the aroma of pine pitch at this sunny spot. This is a good place to pause for a snack or just to listen to the whooshing sound of the wind through the pine boughs. You may also hear the comical trumpeting of tiny red-breasted nuthatches as they creep headfirst down the corrugated conifer trunks.

Leave the gas line and follow the wide path right through woods with tall mountain laurel to a T junction. Turning either direction will lead you in only a few moments to the shores of a picturesque unnamed pond bordered by blooming goldenrods and asters in late summer. The goldenrods literally buzz with honeybees gathering nectar and pollen. On our September visit a big powerful **northern goshawk** streaked across the blue sky, alternating wing flaps and glides. We also saw a sharp-shinned hawk, the smallest of the goshawk's bird-eating relatives.

An informal path skirts the shoreline. At the marshy southern end of the pond is an old beaver lodge. Ruby-throated hummingbirds dart about keying in on orange and red tubular flowers such as spotted touch-me-not where nectar, rich in carbohydrates, and minute insects, rich in protein, lurk. They must fatten up prior to their fall migration flight to Mexico and Central America. It is truly amazing that these creatures, weighing only three grams, are capable of flying nonstop across the Gulf of Mexico's 500 miles of open water! **Monarch butterflies** are also on the move, and goldenrod flowers provide them with the fatty nectar that fuels them on their 2,500-mile migratory flight to the volcanic mountains of central Mexico.

In late summer **bottle** (closed) **gentians** and slender gerardia flower in the damp soil near the north end of the pond. The aptly named gentians, whose clustered blossoms never truly open, are a beautiful blue violet. The gerardia flowers are purplish pink and delicate.

At the far right or north end of the pond where the earthen dam is situated, check out the flowage emerging below the dam, right, for pleasing views of beaver habitat and abundant aquatic life. Beavers have constructed a lodge here and it makes a handy platform from which to scan the dark water. There is a great concentration of **red-spotted newts** here. Within a circular area, perhaps eight feet in diameter, I counted fully 40 of the three-inch-long aquatic salamanders! Red-spotted newts are yellowish green and have six red spots on each flank. Their tails are flattened vertically and provide the propulsion that powers them through the water. Their food consists of aquatic insects, worms, and similar fare, but they are prey to few creatures owing to their toxic skins.

Back on the trail, walk along the top of the dam and soon reach a T intersection. Turn right. This car track will

The flowage below the earthen dam of an unnamed pond has been dammed by beavers, creating excellent habitat for red-spotted newts and other wildlife.

take you to a gate and paved West Hartland Road in about 150 yards. Cross the road, and walk to the right about 250 feet to reach the former homesite. Ancient, gnarled apple trees no longer produce a crop for humans, but deer, raccoons, opossums, squirrels, and other creatures still relish the fallen fruit. At the center of the open area, turn right and follow the car track entering the woods about 100 feet in front of you. The trail proceeds through a pine grove and roughly parallels West Hartland Road. Follow the path to where another trail enters from the left, also marked with blue triangular blazes.

Turn left onto this trail for a short detour to two small, picturesque beaver ponds situated along Halfway Brook. Two beaver dams are easily seen here. In summer Canada warblers nest in the bordering shrubbery.

To return to your car, double back to the last trail junction where you turned left and stay left, which will take you through towering white pines with an understory of hemlock and beech. Just after reaching an old stone wall, the trail swings right and follows Halfway Brook downstream back to your vehicle along West Hartland Road. Alternately, you can walk directly back to your car along Hartland Road from the gated car track (turn right) beyond the unnamed pond, a distance of just a bit more than 0.3 mile.

Getting There

From the junction of Routes 57 and 189 in Granville, travel west on Route 57 for almost 7.0 miles to West Hartland Road on the left. Pass Hartland Hollow Road on the left at about 6.0 miles—do not turn here. Instead, turn left onto West Hartland Road, which has rough pavement but is easily passable, and follow it for 2.1 miles south to the dirt turnout area on the right, opposite the camping area and millpond. Drinking water and rest rooms are available here. The trail begins at the far end of the pond, diagonally across the road.

Hours are dawn to dusk, except for campers. There is no entrance fee; there is a two-dollar fee to park in the picnic area; camping is four dollars per night.

—R.L.

The Meadows
(Stebbins Wildlife Refuge and Long-
meadow Conservation Land)
Longmeadow

800 acres

- 3 miles
- 2.5 hours
- medium

The low-lying land along the **Connecticut River** in Longmeadow is where my love of the outdoors first blossomed. It has everything a young person (or an adult) needs for outdoor adventure: meadows, streams, ponds, woods, and New England's longest river, the Connecticut. This large **floodplain** is considered among the **best birding** spots in the Pioneer Valley. Waterfowl migrating along the Atlantic flyway (a primary migration route along the eastern seaboard) use the area as a resting and feeding spot.

A combination of Longmeadow Conservation Land and property owned by the Fanny Stebbins Wildlife Refuge comprise the Meadows. The Allen Bird Club and the town of Longmeadow have been instrumental in protecting the area. Some of the acreage is used for agriculture, just as it has been since the town was first settled

The Meadows

Connecticut River

cove

field

Sherwood
Section
(evergreens)

West Road

field

Raspberry Brook

Longmeadow Br.

field

pond

P Pond Side Rd.

field

Bark Haul Rd.

N

500 feet

in 1644. The rich flats of the river's floodplain are among the most fertile fields in all of New England.

Begin by following the trail westward into the woods of oak and maple, directly opposite the end of Bark Haul Road. (All of the trails at the meadow are flat, making walking very easy.) You will soon pass a small pond on the right. My brother, Bob, has walked the Meadows almost daily for the last seven years. He frequently observes great blue herons, green-backed herons, and kingfishers here. He also tells me that coyotes are sometimes seen crossing the trail ahead.

In about five minutes you will cross railroad tracks (which are active) and soon arrive at a four-way intersection near an area of the Meadows called the Sherwood Section. If you follow the path straight ahead you will come to a plantation of spruce and pine. Be on the lookout for cottontails, ruffed grouse, and red fox. The evergreens here give one the feeling of being in a magical, mysterious place where titmice, chickadees, and blue jays stay protected from the winter's wind.

From the plantation, it is possible to leave the trail and make your way west to reach the Connecticut River. Enormous trees grow in the dark soil (which is constantly enriched by the flooding river), and there is little undergrowth as you make your way to the mighty Connecticut. The river starts its 409-mile journey in northern New Hampshire at the Canadian border and flows south to Long Island Sound. In all those miles, this section in Longmeadow is the river's widest at 2,100 feet.

Another way to gain access to the river is by returning to the four-way intersection and going north on the trail called West Road. In a short walk you will reach **Longmeadow Brook.** Just before the brook, a trail on the left will take you toward the river. Longmeadow Brook is an interesting stream, with a few trout, lots of bullhead, and, occasionally in the spring, **lamprey eels** that make their way from the river into the brook to spawn. As a boy, I remember catching the eels. Up to three feet long, they have a distinctive round mouth that acts as a sucking organ. They use their mouth and rows of tiny teeth to latch onto other fish and literally suck the life from them. Long ago lampreys were used as food in New England, and smoked eels were considered a delicacy!

Continue by following the West Road Trail to the south. You will first pass through woods and wetlands, then through fields frequented by white-tailed deer. Owls, such as the barred owl and great horned owl, hunt the woods and fields at night.

When you reach the end of the fields (about 15 minutes from Longmeadow Brook), you will see a sign for the Eliot Section. Follow the path near the sign in a southwest direction through the woods (to the rear of the sign). When you reach wetlands on your left, look closely through the undergrowth and you will see where **beaver** have gnawed down some trees. It's just a short

A well-gnawed stump shows the work of beaver to a young explorer.

walk from here to **"the cove."** Bear left when the trail you are on intersects another, and this will bring you to where Raspberry Brook flows into the cove.

All sorts of birds can be found by the backwater during the warm-weather months: herons, blue-winged teal, cormorant, sanderlings, great egrets, even osprey. **Carp,** a fish introduced to America from Asia, are also found in the cove. The carp is a relative of the goldfish but often grows to 20 pounds. I recall many times seeing (and catching) some of these monsters when the fish would get stranded in small pools in the Meadows after the spring floodwaters receded. Sportsmen consider the carp a trash fish, but battling a 20-pound fish on light tackle—no matter what the species—is a lot of fun!

During low-water periods, it is possible to cross Raspberry Brook and head east along a ridge on a path called the Knoll Trail. This trail crosses the railroad tracks, angles to the north, and then angles west before connecting with Pondside Road. This walk does not cross Raspberry Brook but instead follows the cove back to the original trail. When you reach the split in the trail, stay left along the cove. You will soon reach an open area by a field. Turn right and you will be back by the Eliot Section sign.

Follow the trail east, keeping the fields on your left and woods to your right, and you will soon recross the train tracks, pass more wetlands, and pass another field. In 10 minutes the trail will intersect with another Turn left to reach your car in another 10-minute walk. You should be able to see the highway far to the right. The **meadow,** also to your right, is a fine birding spot.

Each season is special at the Meadows. Wildlife is active in the summer. Autumn's crisp days mean few mosquitoes and good walking conditions. The flat trails are excellent for cross-country skiing in the winter, and birding is super in the spring. My favorite time is early spring—when migrating waterfowl and wading birds return and mosquitoes are few. (Remember to wear boots after heavy rains as the trails get quite muddy.)

Getting There

From I-91 take Exit 1 (Longmeadow) and follow Route 5 south through town for about 3.0 miles (passing the beautiful town green) and look for Bark Haul Road on your right. Follow Bark Haul Road to where it ends at Pondside Road (about half a mile), and park by the welcome sign.

Open year-round, seven days a week, no admission fee, no rest rooms.

—M.T.

Laughing Brook Education Center and Wildlife Sanctuary
Hampden
354 acres

- **2.2 miles**
- **2.5 hours**
- **easy**

Pleasant upland woods of oak and pine, babbling brooks, well-marked trails, and fine interpretive facilities characterize this attractive Massachusetts Audubon Society property located just two miles north of the Connecticut border. Numerous old stone walls tell of a time long ago when this land was predominantly open pasture. One path now leads through maturing forest to a big glacial erratic called Split Boulder that is a favorite with children. Hills are mostly moderate and you'll find the walking fairly easy.

The floodplain environment along the sanctuary's three watercourses provides the right conditions for the state-listed wood turtle, as well as mink and belted kingfisher. Complementing the interesting natural communities are numerous wooden viewing platforms, some roofed, and an extensive area of native animal exhibits housed in naturalistic outdoor settings.

Laughing Brook

Half-way Sign

Glacial Trail

red oak
with 7 trunks

erratic

Striped Chipmunk Tr.

Circle of the Season

Glacial Trail

Laughing Brook

Pond Trail

Main Street

P Laughing
Brook Tr.

N

This property was owned previously by naturalist and childrens' storyteller Thornton W. Burgess, who lived here from 1928 until his death in 1965. The Burgess home, dubbed the Storytellers House, is now open by appointment. It is located along Main Street just west of the education center. Many of the sanctuary's natural features and wildlife were immortalized in Burgess's writings. Laughing Brook itself is the storyteller's name for East Brook, which flows northeast to southwest through the southern part of the property. The society purchased the original lands to create the sanctuary in 1966.

Combining several well-maintained trails into a 2.2-mile loop will let you experience the seldom visited "backcountry" of the sanctuary. From the parking lot, enter the education center and register. Interpretive leaflets and a bird checklist are available here as well as rest rooms. After exiting the building to the rear (check the bird feeders out back), turn left at the visitor information board, after picking up an interpretive trail map. Follow the Pond Trail along the shrubby margin of an artificial pond. The ornamental shrubs may be full of birds, especially during spring and fall migration seasons. Turn left onto Laughing Brook Trail, which parallels its namesake. Laughing Brook (East Brook) is well named. Its murmurings are—with a little imagination—reminiscent of giggling laughter. Soon cross the brook on a bridge and walk up a slight slope to a cluster of buildings. The largest of these is the former Burgess home.

Glacial Trail begins here. Climb steps to a point 20 feet or more above Laughing Brook. Walk through dry oak woodland and turn left at a Trail Closed sign. Below the oaks—both white and red—small white pines, lowbush blueberry, and black cherry make up the shrub layer. Bracken fern is common, and beneath it soft hair-cap moss and two clubmosses—princess pine and ground cedar—thrive. The powdery mass of spores from clubmosses were once used to create the explosive flash used in early flash photography! Blue jays, bold and noisy except during nesting season, are ubiquitous in the oak woodlands. Abundant acorn crops feed a wide array of wildlife including chipmunks, squirrels, and deer.

Some of the oaks, especially those left standing along stone walls, are quite large. **White oak** can be distinguished from red oak by its flakier, light gray bark and its round-lobed leaves. Its acorns are also sweeter—containing less bitter tannic acid than those of red and black oaks. The trail swings right and then left, passing by a moist area on the right. Cross the wettest section on a short boardwalk, where water-loving ferns—interrupted, sensitive, and royal—thrive, and pass by a stand of young eastern hemlocks. It was near this wet area that my wife, Chris, and I were surprised to see a big brown bat winging through the oak woods late one morning in early October. In addition to choosing attics and barns for its daytime roosts, this bat also uses large hollow trees. Soon this chocolate brown mammal, with a 10-inch wingspan, will retire to its hibernation site for a six-month sleep—not to reemerge until flying insects once again provide food for it next April.

Where the trail splits at #18 (Striped Chipmunk Trail), stay left on Glacial Trail. You'll pass a cluster of glacial boulders, dropped by the retreating ice, on your right. This forest is different—the soil is wetter and richer in organic matter and it supports different tree species. Sugar maple is more abundant here; in autumn its leaves turn bright yellow. Safely out of sight by day—usually under decaying logs and occasionally under rocks—are three-inch-long **red-backed salamanders** (though often gray). I found 13 on our early October walk.

Soon the trail splits again at #19—stay to the left. The trail descends slightly here and passes rock walls and big, spreading white pines that indicate this was once pastureland. Pines that grow to maturity in woodlands usually exhibit long, straight, single trunks, but those growing in a sunny, recently abandoned pasture have the liberty of growing outward as well as upward. The trail then proceeds through a dry young forest of white pine, birch, and red oak. Hop hornbeam is a major understory tree of these woodlands; the seedpods bear a resemblance to hops. Its small size and thin, brown flaky bark make it quite easy to identify. The tufted titmouse, which has expanded its range northward over the past 50 years, and white-breasted nuthatch are year-round residents. Listen for the nuthatch's nasal "yank-yank" and "wer-wer-wer-wer" calls.

Descend to a rock wall and, turning right, follow along the rock wall on the left through rich woods of oak and maple with a luxuriant growth of Christmas fern (with a bit of imagination, each leaflet looks something like a tiny Christmas stocking). Follow the path slightly up into a dimly lit hemlock stand; look to your left at the massive trunks of two skeletal oak giants known as the **Twin Oaks.** Although long dead, these monoliths provide refuge and den sites to raccoons, bats, flying squirrels, screech owls, and other wildlife.

The trail now swings right and heads uphill through hemlocks, red maples, and red oaks. Little grows in the deep shade. Cross a low rock wall and descend gradually; a tiny Halfway sign sits just above the ground on the left. Beyond this point, enter a hemlock stand of tall straight trees growing on a shaded slope that drops away to Big Brook at a distance to the left. Ahead cross stone walls twice more. Brown creepers hitch up tree trunks, pausing to remove tiny insects and spiders from bark crevices with their thin, down-curved bills, while downy and hairy woodpeckers probe and chisel for insects beneath the bark surface.

At a very large red oak, cross a stone wall and walk through oak/hickory (pignut and shagbark) woods, which soon become oak/maple woods. Some sizable black birches grow here as you pass by a rock outcrop on the left. The ledges are adorned with quite a growth of leafy brown lichens called rock tripe that become green and pliable after absorbing moisture from rain, fog, and dew. This is the highest elevation along the trail. Watch for a red oak with seven trunks, two of which are dead, on your left. The dominant terminal bud was killed early in its life, enabling the other buds to develop shoots to eventually produce this multitrunked form.

The path swings right and then left and descends gradually. Soon you'll reach the intersection you passed before (#19); continue straight to #18, where you'll turn left onto Striped Chipmunk Trail. The trail will take you through an area of gray boulders and past a 10-foot rock ledge, left, that contains horizontal crevices. A bit farther along, left, through pine/oak/maple woods is an isolated erratic some 20 feet long. The small, leathery fronds of rock-loving common polypody fern grow in the thin soil that has collected atop the boulders. Turn left onto the Circle of the Seasons Trail, once an old wood road.

If you wish to see the **Split Boulder**, turn right instead and walk a short distance to a side trail, left, that takes you up a slight rise to the 10-foot-wide by 25-foot-long, wedge-shaped granite glacial erratic. It sits amid a forest of white pine, red oak, hemlock, and a few maples. You might decide to stop and have lunch here as we did. Children find the boulder irresistible for climbing.

When ready, backtrack to the junction of Striped Chipmunk and Circle of the Seasons Trails, and continue straight ahead. Pass the end of a stone wall and the sanctuary boundary, left, and enter a grove of young, straight-boled white pines; thick green patches of pine seedlings cover the forest floor. White pine seeds are winged and disseminated by the wind. White pine, which requires bright sunlight, is one of the first tree species to colonize open ground.

A stone wall parallels the path to a big white oak. Turn left and then pass a big white pine on the right. White oak acorns mature in fall of their first year, whereas red and black oak require two years to mature. If you're here in fall of a good "mast" year, your walk will be punctuated by the nearly constant sound of acorns dropping upon the recently fallen leaves; the ground may be littered with them. Proceed gradually downhill through hemlocks and watch for a small wet depression on the right where spongy, silvery green sphagnum moss grows. This may be the site of a vernal pool that hosts congregations of breeding salamanders in early spring.

Rimmed by fall foliage, a small pond near the education center is a good place to observe birds and other wildlife year-round.

The trail then turns right and brings you to Laughing Brook. The shallow depth and the gravel and rock bottom give rise to the gurgling soliloquy that Burgess so loved. You can also hear noise from Glendale Road. A more natural but rhythmically monotonous sound is made by **true katydids** up in the trees. Their characteristic loud "Katy-did, Katy-didn't" calls can't be missed. The insects rub their wings together to "sing"; the song has territorial and courtship implications.

You'll soon pass a large white pine on the left and cross a small seepage area where hemlocks, maples, and oaks line the brook banks. White pines often attract carpenter ants, and pileated woodpeckers are carpenter ant specialists—finding and chiseling out huge rectangular cavities to get at the ants. Far from damaging the tree, the big red-crested woodpecker simply practices the fine art of the tree surgeon by removing the injurious ants and the dead tissue.

Stop along the sandy banks of the brook to look for signs of nocturnal forest life. Tracks of white-tailed deer that have come to the brook to drink are usually visible in the soft wet sand. Watch, too, for small dark brown scats of semiaquatic predators such as mink. When bounding, **mink** leave paired tracks about 12 to 18 inches apart. Continue past the junction of the very short Forest Trail on the right. The trail then swings right for a very nice view of East Brook and a big boulder (another glacial erratic) on the opposite bank.

Soon you'll join the other end of Circle of the Seasons Trail—continue straight along the brook. The trail then moves away from the brook temporarily and returns to cross it later. Cross the brook over the wide wooden bridge. From the bridge, you can get a good look down into the clear water. Head back toward the pond and the education center; notice lots of planted autumn olive. The juicy red berries are eaten by birds. Check out the shrubs for northern cardinal, American robin, gray catbird, and house finch. The pond itself contains tiny fish, tadpoles, and aquatic insects. Check the skies for big, black, teetering turkey vultures.

Several other short paths are located on the opposite side of Main Street—on both sides of the Scantic River—from the parking area.

Getting There

From I-91 in Springfield take Exit 2 (northbound) or Exit 4 (southbound) onto Route 83 (Route 83 becomes Sumner Avenue). Follow Sumner Avenue east for 3.6 miles and bear right on Allen Street. Continue on Allen Street for 4.7 miles into Hampden and make a left turn at the traffic light onto Main Street. Follow Main Street for 2.0 miles to the large gravel parking area and education center on the left.

Hours are 10:00 A.M. to 4:00 P.M., Tuesday through Saturday, and 12:30 P.M. to 4:00 P.M. on Sundays and Monday holidays. Trails open dawn to dusk. Admission fees are three dollars for nonmember adults, two dollars for children three to fifteen and persons sixty-five and over; free for children under three and members of Massachusetts Audubon Society. The facility is wheelchair-accessible and rest rooms are available. There is a regular year-round schedule of public education programs available from the center. Dogs, firearms, alcoholic beverages, and vehicles are prohibited.

—R.L.

Quick Reference Chart:

Region	Hike	Page Number	Difficulty Level (for children)	Distance (miles RT)
Middlesex and Worcester Counties	Groton Place and Sabine Woods	1	easy	2.5
	Flat Rock Wildlife Sanctuary	7	moderate	1.5
	Lincoln Woods	13	easy	1.0
	Wachusett Mtn. State Reservation	18	challenging	1.5
	Broad Meadow Brook Wildlife Sanctuary	25	easy	2.5
	Purgatory Chasm State Reservation	31	moderate	.5
	Blackstone River and Canal Heritage State Park	36	moderate	3.0
	Douglas State Forest	42	easy	1.0
	Royalston Falls	47	easy/mod.	3.0
	Jacobs Hill Reservation	52	moderate	2.5
	Doane's Falls	58	easy	1.0
	Elliot Laurel Reservation	64	easy	1.0
	Bear's Den	70	easy	.375
	North Common Meadow	75	easy	1.25

*Area Manager: A=Audubon; T=Trustees; SP=State Park; O=Other

Walks and Highlights

River or Brook	Falls or Gorge	Lake or Pond	Scenic Vista	Rocky Ledges	Wooden Bridges	Special Geology	Area*
✔							O
			✔				A
						✔	A
			✔				SP
✔							A
				✔		✔	SP
✔	✔	✔	✔	✔			SP
		✔				✔	SP
✔	✔						T
✔	✔	✔	✔	✔			T
✔	✔	✔					T
				✔			T
✔	✔			✔			T
		✔					T

Region	Hike	Page Number	Difficulty Level (for children)	Distance (miles RT)
Middlesex and Worcester Counties	Swift River Reservation	81	moderate	1.75
	Quabbin Reservoir Gate 45	87	moderate	5.0
	Rock House Reservation	95	easy	1.5
	Tantiusques Reservation	102	easy	1.75
Franklin County	Mt. Grace State Forest	107	difficult	2.8
	Northfield Mountain	114	moderate	4.5
	Erving State Forest	123	easy	0.9
	Wendell State Forest	130	easy	1.4
	Mt. Sugarloaf	138	difficult	2.2
	High Ledges Wildlife Sanctuary	144	moderate	1.7
	Bear Swamp Reservation	150	moderate	2.5
	Chapelbrook Reservation	158	moderate	1.75
	D.A.R. State Forest	163	moderate	2.5
	Kenneth Dubuque Memorial State Forest	170	moderate	4.5
	Mohawk Trail State Forest	178	difficult	4.0

*Area Manager: A=Audubon; T=Trustees;
SP=State Park; O=Other

River or Brook	Falls or Gorge	Lake or Pond	Scenic Vista	Rocky Ledges	Wooden Bridges	Special Geology	Area*
✔			✔	✔			T
✔		✔					O
		✔	✔	✔		✔	T
				✔			T
✔			✔				SP
		✔	✔	✔		✔	O
✔		✔	✔	✔			SP
✔		✔		✔			SP
			✔	✔		✔	SP
✔		✔	✔	✔			A
✔		✔	✔	✔			T
✔	✔		✔	✔			T
		✔	✔				SP
✔		✔					SP
✔			✔	✔			SP

Region	Hike	Page Number	Difficulty Level (for children)	Distance (miles RT)
Hampshire and Hampden Counties	Buffam Falls Conservation Area	186	easy	1.0
	William Cullen Bryant Homestead	191	easy	0.9
	Chesterfield Gorge	197	easy	3.0
	Glendale Falls Reservation	204	moderate	1.2
	Arcadia Wildlife Sanctuary	210	easy	1.75
	Joseph Allen Skinner State Park	215	difficult	1.75
	Holyoke Range State Park	223	moderate	2.75
	Mt. Tom State Reservation	232	difficult	4.5
	Sanderson Brook Falls	240	easy	2.0
	Tolland State Forest	246	moderate	3.3
	Granville State Forest	255	moderate	2.0
	The Meadows	262	moderate	3.0
	Laughing Brook Educ. Ctr. and W.S.	268	easy	2.2

***Area Manager: A=Audubon; T=Trustees;
SP=State Park; O=Other**

River or Brook	Falls or Gorge	Lake or Pond	Scenic Vista	Rocky Ledges	Wooden Bridges	Special Geology	Area*
✔	✔			✔			O
✔			✔				T
✔	✔		✔			✔	T
✔	✔		✔	✔			T
✔		✔	✔			✔	A
			✔	✔		✔	SP
			✔	✔		✔	SP
			✔	✔		✔	SP
✔	✔			✔			SP
✔		✔	✔				SP
✔	✔	✔					SP
✔		✔					O
✔		✔		✔	✔	✔	A

Recommended References and Reading

Birding by Ear: *Guide to Bird Song Identification,* and *More Birding by Ear*: *Eastern and Central*, three CDs or cassettes by Richard K. Walton and Robert W. Lawson. Peterson Field Guides. Published by Houghton Mifflin Company. 1989, 1994. Both teach songs of common species by comparison method.

Changes in the Land; Indians, Colonists, and the Ecology of New England by William Cronon. Published by Hill and Wang. 1983. An interesting melding of human and natural history.

The Changing Face of New England by Betty Flanders Thomson. Published by Houghton Mifflin Company. 1977. An ecological and land-use perspective.

Golden Guides published by Golden Press. Titles include: Pond Life, Insects, Butterflies and Moths, Mammals, Birds, Nonflowering Plants, Trees, Reptiles and Amphibians, and Rocks and Minerals. Excellent introductory identification guides.

A Guide to New England's Landscape by Neil Jorgensen. Published by Globe Pequot Press. 1977. A geologic perspective.

Newcomb's Wildflower Guide by Lawrence Newcomb. Published by Little, Brown and Company. 1977. Guide utilizes keys to identification; wonderful illustrations.

Peterson Field Guides published by Houghton Mifflin Company. Titles include: Eastern Birds, Mammals, Animal Tracks, Reptiles and Amphibians (Eastern and Central), Eastern Butterflies, Trees and Shrubs, Wildflowers, Ferns, and Eastern Forests. All are excellent.

A Sierra Club Naturalist's Guide to Southern New England by Neil Jorgensen. Published by Sierra Club Books. 1978. An ecological examination of natural communities and their characteristic plants and animals.

Stokes Nature Guides published by Little, Brown and Company. Titles include: Nature in Winter; Bird Behavior I, II, and III; Animal Tracking and Behavior; Observing Insect Lives; and Amphibians and Reptiles. These are behavior oriented and excellent.

Wild Mammals of New England by Alfred J. Godin. Published by the Johns Hopkins University Press. 1977. The most complete work on the region's mammal life.

About the Authors

RENÉ LAUBACH has been director of Massachusetts Audubon Society's Berkshire Wildlife Sanctuaries since 1985. Growing up in Michigan, he spent 14 years in museum work before assuming his current position. Since moving to western Massachusetts, René has been active in the Hoffmann Bird Club, serving as president in 1989 and 1990. He resides in the Berkshire hill town of Becket and sits on its Conservation Commission. He is also on the Executive Committee of the Mt. Greylock Protective Association. Both René and his wife are avid, licensed bird banders and walkers. Together they completed the Massachusetts portion of the Appalachian Trail in 1991.

Laubach has authored articles for the Massachusetts Audubon Society's *Sanctuary* magazine and several scientific journals dealing with birds. With his wife, Christyna, and John B. Bowles, he wrote *A Guide to the Bats of Iowa,* published by the Iowa Department of Natural Resources. He is also author of *A Guide to Natural Places in the Berkshire Hills.* When not exploring Massachusetts, he enjoys leading natural history tours to the American Southwest and Latin America.

MICHAEL TOUGIAS is a native New Englander who writes on a wide range of topics including history, nature, gardening, and travel. His travel columns appear in the Springfield *Union News, Patriot Ledger, Middlesex News, Sun Chronicle,* and other newspapers. In his free time he enjoys hiking with his family, fishing, canoeing, and reading. When not exploring Massachusetts, he spends time at his rustic cabin in northern Vermont.

Tougias frequently gives slide presentations about special historic and natural places in New England. Whenever possible he volunteers for conservation work in an effort to save more open spaces. He is the author of *Nature Walks in Eastern Massachusetts, Quiet Places in Massachusetts, Autumn Trails, A Taunton River Journey, The Hidden Charles,* and *Country Roads of Massachusetts.* He has also published recreation maps and guides to Cape Cod, hidden Quabbin, Cape Ann, and the southern Berkshires. Tougias's first novel, *Until I Have No Country* (about King Philip's War), will be released in the fall of 1996. If you are interested in his publications or slide presentations, send a self-addressed stamped envelope to M. Tougias, PO Box 72, Norfolk, MA 02056.

About the AMC

The Appalachian Mountain Club pursues an active conservation agenda while encouraging responsible recreation. Founded in 1876, the club has been at the forefront of the environmental protection movement. Our philosophy is that successful long-term conservation depends on firsthand experience of the natural environment. AMC's 67,000 members pursue interests in hiking, canoeing, skiing, walking, rock climbing, bicycling, camping, kayaking, and backpacking, and—at the same time—help safeguard the environment.

The most recent efforts in the AMC Conservation program include river protection, Northern Forest lands policy, Sterling Forest (NY) preservation, and support for the Clean Air Act. The AMC depends upon its active members and grassroots supporters to promote this conservation agenda.

The AMC's Education department offers members and the general public a wide range of workshops, from introductory camping to the intensive Mountain Leadership School taught on the trails of the White Mountains. In addition, volunteers in each chapter lead hundreds of outdoor activities and excursions and offer introductory instruction in backcountry sports.

The AMC's Research department focuses on the forces affecting the ecosystem, including ozone levels, acid rain and fog, climate change, rare flora and habitat protection, and air quality and visibility.

Another facet of the AMC is the Trails program, which maintains more than 1,400 miles of trail (including 350 miles of the Appalachian Trail) and more than 50 shelters in the Northeast. Through a coordinated effort of volunteers, seasonal crews, and program staff, the AMC contributes more than 10,000 hours of public service work each summer in the area from Washington, D.C., to Maine.

In addition to supporting our work by becoming an AMC member, hikers can donate time as volunteers. For more information on these public service volunteer opportunities, contact the AMC Trails Program, Pinkham Notch Visitor Center, PO Box 298, Gorham NH 03581; 603-466-2721.

The club operates eight alpine huts in the White Mountains that provide shelter, bunks and blankets, and hearty meals for hikers. Pinkham Notch Visitor Center, at the foot of Mt. Washington, is base camp to the adventurous and the ideal location for individuals and families new to outdoor recreation. Comfortable bunk rooms, mountain hospitality, and home-cooked, family-style meals make Pinkham Notch Visitor Center a fun and affordable choice for lodging. For reservations, call 603-466-2727.

The AMC's offices in Boston and at Pinkham Notch Visitor Center stock the entire line of AMC publications, as well as other trail and river guides, maps, reference materials, and the latest articles on conservation issues. Guidebooks and other AMC gifts can be ordered by calling 800-262-4455 or by writing AMC, PO Box 298, Gorham, NH 03581. Also available from the bookstore or by subscription is *Appalachia,* the country's oldest mountaineering and conservation journal.

Alphabetical Listing of Areas

Index